Praise for *Searching for Sunday*

As you read *Searching for Sunday*, you will feel that you are being breathed into, not just by Held Evans, but also I think, by the Holy Spirit, who felt very near, right at hand, as I was turning these pages.

— Lauren F. Winner, author of *Wearing God* and *Still: Notes on a Mid-faith Crisis*

Rachel Held Evans burst onto the scene a few years ago as a young writer with great promise. In *Searching for Sunday*, she fulfills that promise, writing with beauty, insight, maturity, humility, and plenty of humor. If you need a book to pastor you, befriend you, pick you up and dust you off, and maybe even give you a spiritual kiss on the cheek and a devotional kick in the pants, you've found it here.

— Brian D. McLaren, author and speaker (brianmclaren.net)

If you're done with church or simply on the verge of throwing in the towel, then please, please, please read this book. It's a brave, wry, and exquisitely penned meditation from someone who knows precisely how you feel. I loved every word.

— Ian Morgan Cron, best-selling author, speaker, and Episcopal priest

Rachel Held Evans has written a spiritual travel guide for religious runaways. She beautifully takes us with her as she leaves home, wanders, questions, suffers, and then returns. But the church she returns to is as true, raw, and beautifully difficult as the writer herself. As someone who has also left, been angered by, missed, then returned to church, I love this book. I love how Rachel doesn't shy away from what's ugly in her search for what's beautiful both in herself and the church.

— Pastor Nadia Bolz-Weber, author of *Pastrix: The Cranky, Beautiful Faith of a Sinner & Saint*

Oh my goodness, this is Rachel's best book yet—and that's saying something. In this beautifully honest, hopefully wry book, Rachel speaks for so many of us. I believe that her hard-fought words will heal many wounds. A must-read for all who love Jesus but struggle with loving or understanding or finding their place in the Church.

— Sarah Bessey, author of *Jesus Feminist* and *Out of Sorts*

Evans has written a zinger of a book. She is grounded in the deep things of faith. She writes in a vivid style and transposes the claims of faith into compelling concrete narrative. Her book is a forceful invitation to reconsider that faith has been misunderstood as a package of certitudes rather than a relationship of fidelity.

— Walter Brueggemann, Columbia Theological Seminary

In *Searching for Sunday*, Rachel's honest and hopeful wrestling tore through my cynicism about the perils of organized religion and touched my heart—reminding me why this heart achingly broken but beautiful Bride is worth the fight.

— Michael Gungor, musician, composer, and author of *The Crowd, the Critic, and the Muse: A Book for Creators*

It is always refreshing to hear the painful truth about the conflicted life of faith from one more recovering American Christian. Yet it is even more poignantly healing to witness how our fitful human, sin-tainted truths can still lead us back to the one Truth that can hold it all. In these pages there is room for sacred doubting and holy tantrums because ultimately the love and grace of God permits us all that room.

— Enuma Okoro, Nigerian-American speaker and award-winning author of *Reluctant Pilgrim: A Moody Somewhat Self-Indulgent Introvert's Search for Spiritual Community*

Searching for Sunday

Loving, Leaving, and Finding the Church

Rachel Held Evans

NELSON
BOOKS

An Imprint of Thomas Nelson

Published in Nashville, Tennessee, by Nelson Books, an imprint of Thomas Nelson. Nelson Books and Thomas Nelson are registered trademarks of HarperCollins Christian Publishing, Inc.

Published in association with the Books & Such Literary Agency, 52 Mission Circle, Suite 122, PMB 170, Santa Rosa, CA 95409-5370, www.booksandsuch.biz.

Thomas Nelson, Inc., titles may be purchased in bulk for educational, business, fundraising, or sales promotional use. For information, please e-mail SpecialMarkets@ ThomasNelson.com.

Unless otherwise noted, Scripture quotations are taken from the Holy Bible, New International Version®, NIV®. Copyright © 1973, 1978, 1984, 2011 by Biblica, Inc.™ Used by permission of Zondervan. All rights reserved worldwide. www.zondervan.com

Scripture quotations marked ESV are from THE ENGLISH STANDARD VERSION. © 2001 by Crossway Bibles, a division of Good News Publishers.

Scripture quotations marked NLT are from *Holy Bible*, New Living Translation. © 1996. Used by permission of Tyndale House Publishers, Inc., Wheaton, Illinois 60189. All rights reserved.

Scripture quotations marked NRSV are from NEW REVISED STANDARD VERSION of the Bible. © 1989 by the Division of Christian Education of the National Council of the Churches of Christ in the U.S.A. All rights reserved.

Library of Congress Control Number: 2014956181

ISBN-13: 978-0-7180-2212-9

Printed in the United States of America

15 16 17 18 19 RRD 10 9 8 7

To Amanda—the little sister I look up to,
and the person who makes me most
hopeful about the future of the church.

And to the community on the blog—I
wrote every word of this book for you.

I prefer a church which is bruised, hurting and dirty because it has been out on the streets, rather than a church which is unhealthy from being confined and from clinging to its own security . . . More than by fear of going astray, my hope is that we will be moved by the fear of remaining shut up within structures which give us a false sense of security, within rules which make us harsh judges, within habits which make us feel safe, while at our door people are starving and Jesus does not tire of saying to us, "Give them something to eat."

—Pope Francis[1]

Contents

IV. Communion

V. Confirmation

VI. Anointing of the Sick

VII. Marriage

Foreword

WHENEVER I WANT TO SCARE MYSELF, I CONSIDER WHAT would happen to the world if Rachel Held Evans stopped writing.

As I tore through the pages in this book, I realized I'd been waiting my whole life for *Searching for Sunday*. The Jesus that Rachel loves fiercely is the same Jesus I fell in love with long ago, before I let my the hypocrisy of the church and my own heart muddle everything up. *Searching for Sunday* helped me forgive the church and myself and fall in love with God all over again. It was as if, over time, road blocks had been set up between me and God and as I read this book I could feel Rachel's words removing them one at a time until by the end of the book I was looking directly at God again.

Rachel's Christianity is a daily discipline of boundless grace–for herself, for the church, for those the church leaves out. The faith she describes in *Searching for Sunday* is less of a club to belong to and more of a current to enter into—a current that continuously carries her toward the people and places she's been taught to fear. Rachel finds herself not only loving these people, but learning that she *is* these people. In *Searching for Sunday*, Rachel convinces us that there is no *them* and *us*; there is only us. This idea of hers is both comforting and slightly terrifying. I have a hunch that comforting and terrifying is exactly what faith should be.

Searching for Sunday is, quite simply, my favorite book by my favorite writer. From now on when people ask me about my faith, I will just hand them this book. Sweet Jesus, I'm grateful for Rachel Held Evans.

— Glennon Doyle Melton
Author of the *New York Times* bestseller *Carry On, Warrior* and founder of Momastery.com and Together Rising

Dawn

I'll tell you how the sun rose a ribbon at a time.

—Emily Dickinson

German theologian Dietrich Bonhoeffer wrote that "the early mornings belong to the Church of the risen Christ. At the break of light it remembers the morning on which death and sin lay prostrate in defeat and new life and salvation were given to mankind."[2]

This comes as unfortunate news for someone like me who can barely remember who she is at the "break of light," much less ponder the theological implications of the resurrection. I'm not exactly what you call a morning person and would, in fact, prefer to be the one lying prostrate in defeat at such an early hour. The halcyon joy of watching the sunrise remains for me just another of the universe's inaccessible gifts, like the northern lights and naturally curly hair. No doubt I would have shooed poor Mary Magdalene away with a soft, pillow-muffled grunt had she asked me to help her bring the burial spices to the tomb that fateful morning two thousand years ago. I'd have slept right through the Main Event.

Religious folks have always had it out for us night owls. My book of hours stipulates that morning prayers be said between 4:30 and 7:30 a.m. How I'm supposed to talk to God at an hour in which I cannot even speak coherently to my husband is beyond me. Yet nearly all the church's most venerated saints were said to be early risers, and growing up, I remember pastors speaking reverently about their morning quiet times, as though God kept strict office hours. Even the world's great cathedrals are built with their entrances on the west side and their altars on the favored east. Old European churchyards, dappled with wind-abraded headstones, still reflect the custom of burying the dead with their feet toward the rising sun as a sign of hope and with the expectation that when Jesus returns to Jerusalem at the Second Coming, the faithful will rise and look him in the eye. One can only hope this will happen sometime after nine o'clock in the morning, eastern standard time.

If early mornings indeed belong to the church, then my generation is sleeping in.

In the United States, 59 percent of young people ages eighteen to twenty-nine with a Christian background have dropped out of church. Among those of us who came of age around the year 2000, a solid quarter claim no religious affiliation at all, making us significantly more disconnected from faith than members of generation X were at a comparable point in their lives and twice as disconnected as baby boomers were as young adults. It is estimated that eight million young adults will leave the church before their thirtieth birthday.[3]

At thirty-two, I only just qualify as a millennial. (Let's just say I still have several episodes of *Friends* saved—on *tape*.) But despite having one foot in generation X, I tend to identify most strongly with the attitudes and ethos of the millennial generation, and because of this, I'm often asked to speak to church leaders about why young adults are leaving the church.

One could write volumes around that question, and, indeed, many have. I can't speak exhaustively about the social and historical currents that shape American religious life or about the forces that draw so many of my peers away from faith altogether. The issues that haunt American evangelicalism are different than those that haunt mainline Protestants, which are different than those that affect Catholic and Episcopal parishes, which are different than those influencing Christianity in the parts of the world where it is actually flourishing—namely, the global South and East.

But I can tell my own story, which studies suggest is an increasingly common one.[4] I can talk about growing up evangelical, about doubting everything I believed about God, about loving, leaving, and longing for church, about searching for it and finding it in unexpected places. And I can share the stories of my friends and readers, people young and old whose comments, letters, and e-mails read like postcards from their own spiritual journeys, dispatches from America's post-Christian frontier. I can't provide the solutions church leaders are looking for, but I can articulate the questions that many in my generation are asking. I can translate some of their angst, some of their hope.

At least that's what I tried to do when I was recently asked to explain to three thousand evangelical youth workers gathered together for a conference in Nashville, Tennessee, why millennials like me are leaving the church.

I told them we're tired of the culture wars, tired of Christianity getting entangled with party politics and power. Millennials want to be known by what we're for, I said, not just what we're against. We don't want to choose between science and religion or between our intellectual integrity and our faith. Instead, we long for our churches to be safe places to doubt, to ask questions, and to tell the truth, even when it's uncomfortable. We want to talk about the tough stuff—biblical interpretation, religious pluralism, sexuality, racial reconciliation, and social justice—but without predetermined conclusions or simplistic answers. We want to bring our whole selves through the church doors, without leaving our hearts and minds behind, without wearing a mask.

I explained that when our gay, lesbian, bisexual, and transgender friends aren't welcome at the table, then we don't feel welcome either, and that not every young adult gets married or has children, so we need to stop building our churches around categories and start building them around people. And I told them that, contrary to popular belief, we can't be won back with hipper worship bands, fancy coffee shops, or pastors who wear skinny jeans. We millennials have been advertised to our entire lives, so we can smell b.s. from a mile away. The church is the last place we want to be sold another product, the last place we want to be entertained.

Millennials aren't looking for a *hipper* Christianity, I said. We're looking for a *truer* Christianity, a more *authentic* Christianity. Like every generation before ours and every generation after, we're looking for Jesus—the same Jesus who can be found in the strange places he's always been found: in bread, in wine, in baptism, in the Word, in suffering, in community, and among the least of these.

No coffee shops or fog machines required.

Of course, I said all this from the center of a giant stage equipped with lights, trampolines, and, indeed, a fog machine. I'm never entirely comfortable at these events—not because my words are unwelcome or untrue, but because I feel so out of my depth delivering them. I'm not a scholar or statistician. I've never led a youth group or pastored a congregation. The truth is, I don't even bother getting out of bed many Sunday mornings, especially on days when I'm not sure I believe in God or when there's an interesting guest on *Meet the Press*. For me, talking about church in front of a bunch of Christians means approaching a microphone and attempting to explain the most important, complicated, beautiful, and heart-wrenching relationship of my life in thirty minutes or less without yelling or crying or saying any cuss words. Sometimes I wish they'd find someone with a bit more emotional distance to give these lectures, someone who doesn't have to break herself open and bleed all over the place every time someone asks, innocently enough, "So where have you been going to church these days?"

Perhaps this is why I didn't want to write this book . . . at least not at first. Oh, I tried to get out of it. I hemmed and hawed and pitched a bunch of alternative proposals to my publisher, hoping the editors might change their minds. It took twice as long to write as I'd planned. I even spilled a fat mug of chai all over my laptop right in the middle of writing the first draft, and, thinking I'd lost half the manuscript, decided that God didn't want me to write a book about church either. (We were able to recover most of the manuscript, but my caps lock still gets stuck from time to time.)

I didn't want to put my church story in print because, the truth is, I still don't know the ending. I am in the adolescence of my faith. There have been slammed doors and rolled eyes and defiant declarations of "I hate you!" hurled at every person or organization that represents the institutionalized church. I am angry and petulant, hopeful and naïve. I am trying to make my own way, but I haven't yet figured out how to do that without exorcising the old one, without shouting it down, declaring my independence, and then running as fast as I can in the opposite direction. Church books are written by people with a plan and ten steps, not by Christians just hanging on by their fingernails.

And yet I am writing. I am writing because I suspect the awkward teenager in the yearbook picture still has something to say about the world, some sort of hope to offer it, if nothing more than a few hundred pages of "me too." I am writing because sometimes we are closer to the truth in our vulnerability than in our safe certainties, and because in spite of all my doubt and insecurity, in spite of my abiding impulse to sleep in on Sunday mornings, I have seen the first few ribbons of dawn's light seep through my bedroom window, and there is a dim, hopeful glow kissing the horizon. Even when I don't believe in church, I believe in resurrection. I believe in the hope of Sunday morning.

It seemed fitting to arrange the book around the sacraments because it was the sacraments that drew me back to church after I'd given up on it. When my faith had become little more than an abstraction, a set of propositions to be affirmed or denied, the tangible, tactile nature of the sacraments invited me to touch, smell, taste, hear, and see God in the stuff of everyday life again. They got God out of my head and into my hands. They reminded me that Christianity isn't meant to simply be believed; it's meant to be lived, shared, eaten, spoken, and enacted in the presence of other people. They reminded me that, try as I may, I can't be a Christian on my own. I need a community. I need the church.

As Barbara Brown Taylor puts it, "in an age of information overload . . . the last thing any of us needs is more information about God. We need the practice of incarnation, by which God saves the lives of those whose intellectual assent has turned them dry as dust, who have run frighteningly low on the bread of life, who are dying to know more God in their bodies. Not more *about* God. More *God*."⁵

So I am telling my church story in seven sections, through the imagery of baptism, confession, holy orders, communion, confirmation, anointing of the sick, and marriage. These are the seven sacraments named by Roman Catholic and Orthodox churches, but one need not consider them the church's only sacraments. I could easily write about the sacrament of pilgrimage, the sacrament of foot washing, the sacrament of the Word, the sacrament of making chicken casseroles, or any number of outward signs of inward grace. My aim in employing these seven sacraments is not theological or ecclesiological, but rather literary. They are the tent pegs anchoring my little tabernacle of a story to the ground. I chose them because they have something of a universal quality, for even in churches that are not expressly sacramental, the truths of the sacraments are generally shared.

The church tells us we are beloved (baptism).
The church tells us we are broken (confession).
The church tells us we are commissioned (holy orders).
The church feeds us (communion).
The church welcomes us (confirmation).
The church anoints us (anointing of the sick).
The church unites us (marriage).

Of course, the church can also lie, injure, damage, and exclude, and this book explores its dark corners as well as its stained-glass splendors. But for a generation that is struggling to make sense of what church is for, I hope these seven mysteries remind us to "taste and see that the LORD is good" (Psalm

34:8) and to maybe not give up. I hope they remind us of how badly we need one another.

I have featured in these pages the stories of churches from a variety of traditions—Baptist, Mennonite, Anglican, Catholic, Pentecostal, nondenominational—and I have drawn heavily from the writings of Christians ranging from Alexander Schmemann (Orthodox), to Nadia Bolz-Weber (Lutheran), to Will Willimon (Methodist), to Sara Miles (Episcopalian). I have included the stories of laypeople and pastors, friends and blog readers, the churched and the unchurched. This is my story, but it is also the story of many others.

This book is entitled *Searching for Sunday*, but it's less about searching for a Sunday *church* and more about searching for Sunday *resurrection*. It's about all the strange ways God brings dead things back to life again. It's about giving up and starting over again. It's about why, even on days when I suspect all this talk of Jesus and resurrection and life everlasting is a bunch of bunk designed to coddle us through an essentially meaningless existence, I should still like to be buried with my feet facing the rising sun.

Just in case.

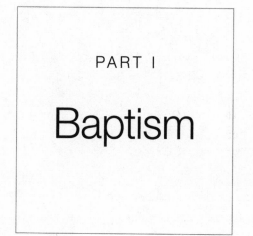

PART I

Baptism

ONE

Water

*. . . by God's word the heavens came into being and
the earth was formed out of water and by water.*

—2 Peter 3:5

In the beginning, the Spirit of God hovered over water.

The water was dark and deep and everywhere, the ancients say, an endless primordial sea.

Then God separated the water, pushing some of it below to make oceans, rivers, dew drops, and springs, and vaulting the rest of the torrents above to be locked behind a glassy firmament, complete with doors that opened for the moon and windows to let out the rain. In ancient Near Eastern cosmology, all of life hung suspended between these waters, vulnerable as a fetus in the womb. With one sigh of the Spirit, the waters could come crashing in and around the earth, drowning its inhabitants in a moment. The story of Noah's flood begins when "the springs of the great deep burst forth, and the floodgates of the heavens were opened" (Genesis 7:11). The God who had separated the waters in the beginning wanted to start over, so God washed the world away.

For people whose survival depended on the inscrutable moods of the Tigris, Euphrates, and Nile, water represented both life and death. Oceans teemed with monsters, unruly spirits, and giant fish that could swallow a man whole. Rivers brimmed with fickle possibility—of yielding crops, of boosting trade, of drying up. Into this world, God spoke the language of water, turning the rivers of enemies into blood, calling forth springs from desert rocks, playing matchmaker around wells, and promising a future in which justice would roll down like water and righteousness like an ever-flowing stream. And the people spoke back, seeking purity of mind and body through ritualistic bathing after birth, death, sex, menstruation, sacrifices, conflicts, and transgressions. "Cleanse me with hyssop, and I will be clean," the poet-king David wrote; "wash me, and I will be whiter than snow" (Psalm 51:7).

It is naïve to think all of these ancient visions must be literal to be true. We know, as our ancestors did, both the danger and necessity of water. Water knits us together in our mothers' wombs, our ghostlike tissue inhaling and exhaling the embryonic fluid that grows our lungs and bones and brains. Water courses through our bodies and makes our planet blue. It is water that lifts cars like leaves when a tsunami rages to shore, water that in a moment can swallow a ship and in eons carve a canyon, water we trawl for like chimps for bugs with billion-dollar equipment scavenging Mars, water we drop on the bald heads of babies to name them children of God, water we torture with and cry with, water that carries the invisible diseases that will kill four thousand children today, water that if warmed just a few degrees more will come crashing in and around the earth and wash us all away.

But just as water carried Moses to his destiny down the Nile, so water carried another baby from a woman's body into an expectant world. Wrapped now in flesh, the God who once hovered over the waters was plunged beneath them at the hands of a wild-eyed wilderness preacher. When God emerged, he spoke of living water that forever satisfies and of being born again. He went fishing and washed his friends' feet. He touched the ceremonially unclean. He spit in the dirt, cast demons into the ocean, and strolled across an angry sea. He got thirsty and he wept.

After the government washed its hands of him, God hung on a cross where blood and water spewed from his side. Like Jonah, he got swallowed up for three days.

Then God beat death. God rose from the depths and breathed air once again. When he found his friends on the shoreline, he told them not to be afraid but to go out and baptize the whole world.

The Spirit that once hovered over the waters had inhabited them. Now every drop is holy.

TWO

Believer's Baptism

All water has a perfect memory and is forever
trying to get back to where it was.

—Toni Morrison

I WAS BAPTIZED BY MY FATHER. HIS PRESENCE BESIDE ME
in the waist-high water of the baptistery marked yet another
perk to having a dad who was ordained but not a pastor, able to
participate in my spiritual life without ruining it. The expectations of the daughter of a Bible college professor are much
laxer than those of a preacher's kid, let me tell you, and mainly
involved gentle suggestions that I redirect some of the questions I asked in Sunday school to the one person in my life who
knew ancient Hebrew and could explain over breakfast exactly
how God managed to create light before the sun.

So I mostly believed my father when he assured me I
wouldn't go to hell for waiting until I was nearly thirteen to get
baptized. *Mostly.* I knew I was pushing the limits of the "age of
accountability," the point at which kids no longer ate for free at

O'Charley's or got into heaven based on their parents' faithfulness, and I knew that some Christians believed you had to get baptized to be saved. In a rude introduction to the realities of denominationalism, I'd been informed by a fifth-grade classmate that even though I'd asked Jesus into my heart when I was in kindergarten, I needed to seal the deal and get baptized quick before a car accident or nasty fall off the tall slide took me straight to the devil.

"My pastor says you have to be baptized with water before you can be baptized by the Spirit," the boy explained, a general practitioner recommending me to a specialist from across the monkey bars. "You should probably get that taken care of."

"Well, my dad went to seminary and he says you don't have to be baptized to go to heaven," I shot back.

(I should mention I attended a Christian elementary school where "my dad's hermeneutic can beat up your dad's hermeneutic" served as legit schoolyard banter.)

A lot of the kids at Parkway Christian Academy went to the Pentecostal church across the street and during prayer-request time delivered numinous accounts of demons sneaking into their bedrooms at night and flashing the lights or flushing the toilets. They took spiritual warfare super-seriously and considered my family liberals for trick-or-treating on Satan's holiday. My father said demons were in the temptation business, not the toilet-flushing business, but his assurances didn't stop me from trembling beneath my covers some nights, afraid to open my eyes and face the thick presence I knew to be a fallen angel looming over my bed, waiting to seize the easy prey of a girl who went trick-or-treating and hadn't bothered to get baptized. By the time I reached the age of accountability, I'd seen enough doctrinal diversity within the church to want to cover my bases, so I began working more questions about baptism into our regular theological conversations around the dinner table, hoping my parents would make an appointment with our pastor. When I learned that some kids got baptized before they even teethed, I bristled with envy.

Our church believed the Bible, so we practiced immersion. Believer's baptism, we called it. Had we lived in sixteenth-century Switzerland, we might have been killed for such a conviction, symbolically drowned or possibly burned by fellow Protestants who considered the "second baptisms" of the radical reformers heretical. (Fun fact: more Christians were martyred by one another in the decades after the Reformation than were martyred by the Roman Empire.[6]) If I'd been born into an Orthodox family, I'd have been submerged as an infant three times over—first in the name of the Father, then in the name of the Son, and then again in the name of the Holy Spirit—before being placed, stunned and sputtering, into the arms of a godparent. If my family had been Catholic, I'd have worn a soft white baptism gown and a priest would have poured holy water over my bald baby head to remit the stain of original sin. If we'd been Mormon, two witnesses would have stood on either side of the font to ensure my entire body was totally submerged in the water. If we'd been Presbyterian, a few sprinkles symbolizing my place in the covenant family of God would do. Fortunately, while disagreements regarding the method of baptism abound, these days Christians prefer giving one another the stink eye over the stake.

I don't think it matters much. Believer's baptism strikes me as something of a misnomer anyway, suggesting far more volition in this circumstance than most of us have. Whether you meet the water as a baby squirming in the arms of a nervous priest, or as an adult plunged into a river by a revivalist preacher, you do it at the hands of those who first welcome you to faith, the people who have—or will—introduce you to Jesus. "In baptism," writes Will Willimon, "the recipient of baptism is just that—recipient. You cannot very well do your own baptism. It is done to you, for you."[7] It's an adoption, not an interview.

The church that adopted me was Southern and evangelical and, consequently, obsessed with college football. Under the leadership of Gene Stallings, the Alabama Crimson Tide was rolling toward its twelfth national championship, so on Sunday mornings after game day, the traditional pews of Bible Chapel in Birmingham were mottled with red and white hair bows, neckties, sports jackets, and blouses—the sacred accoutrements of Alabama's second religion (or first, depending on who you ask).[8] There were a few Auburn fans in attendance, but they were nearly as elusive as Democrats. A single Italian family, the Marinos, comprised our ethnic diversity. We gathered together beneath a vaulted ceiling of Alabama pine and, like good Protestants, faced a heavy, unadorned pulpit. It was the '80s, so all my earliest memories of Jesus smell like hair spray.

At the time, I had no concept of evangelicalism as a unique, relatively recent expression of Christianity with roots in eighteenth-century Pietism and the American Great Awakenings. Instead I understood *evangelical* to be an adjective synonymous with "real" or "authentic." There were *Christians*, and then there were *evangelical Christians* like us. Only evangelicals were assured salvation. Everyone else was lukewarm and in danger of being spewed out of God's mouth. Our Catholic neighbors were doomed. Nine-hundred miles away, in Princeton, New Jersey, my future husband was winning trophies in the pinewood derby at Montgomery Evangelical Free Church, which for many years he took to mean was a church free of evangelicals, like sugar-free gum. "But aren't evangelicals the good guys?" he remembers asking his mother. How early we learn to identify our tribes.

Our pastor at Bible Chapel—Pastor George—hailed from New Orleans and let you know it with his booming bayou drawl and purple-and-gold striped ties. Stout, playful, and a true raconteur, his favorite sermon illustrations involved drawn-out stories about fish that got away and gators that nearly ate him alive. My mother would sometimes tease him after the service by saying he was as bad as the Gideons, a group of Bible distributors whose tales of miraculous Bible encounters (there was one about a dog who delivered a tattered Gideon Bible to his homeless owner before dying in his arms) she never really believed.

I missed all but a few of Pastor George's famous sermons because my little sister, Amanda, and I were usually dismissed to children's church after announcements, hymns, and special music. My mother is a third-generation elementary schoolteacher and staunch defender of age-appropriate education with little tolerance for people who leave their kids in the service to doodle on the bulletin while a preacher drones on and on about substitutionary atonement. Having been forced to do just that as a child—often three to four times a week at a strict independent Baptist church—she made it clear to my father and to anyone else who asked that we only attended church twice a week: once on Sunday morning and once on Wednesday nights. We were conservatives, not legalists.

But even as a kid you learn pretty quick that church doesn't start and stop with the hours of service posted on the church sign. No, church dragged on like the last hour of the school day as we waited in the hot car with Dad for Mom to finish socializing in the fellowship hall. Church lingered long into the gold-tinted Sunday afternoons when Amanda and I gamboled around the house, stripped down to our white slips like little brides. Church showed up at the front door with a chicken casserole when the whole family was down with the flu and called after midnight to ask for prayer and to cry. It gossiped in the pickup line at school and babysat us on Friday nights. It teased me and tugged at my pigtails and taught me how to sing. Church threw Dad a big surprise party for his fortieth birthday and let me in on the secret ahead of time. Church came to me far more than I went to it, and I'm glad.

Given the normal Held family schedule, it felt strange to pull into the long, tree-lined gravel driveway of Bible Chapel on an early Sunday evening for our baptism service, Amanda and I quiet and nervous and strapped in to the backseat of our Chevy Caprice. Part of the reason we delayed my baptism was so she and I could be baptized on the same day, which I considered yet another example of Amanda's uncanny capacity for staying ahead of me in maturity, even though I have three years on her age. Precocious and dimpled, with olive skin and deep, mossy eyes that to this day instantly betray whatever joy or heartache is working through her heart, Amanda could pry a smile out of even the crustiest church elder. She was trusting, impressionable, transparent, and good—the last person in the world anyone ever wanted to make cry.

Pastor George called Amanda Miss AWANA because she so excelled at the Bible memorization classes we attended every Wednesday night. AWANA, which stands for Approved Workmen Are Not Ashamed, is far less socialist than it sounds and in fact involved earning badges and pins for the successful recitation of the verses printed in our spiral booklets. The whole enterprise smelled deliciously of sugar cookies and the freshly laminated paper in our memorization books, and Amanda carried the scent home with her weekly, along with armfuls of ribbons and trophies. But rather than bragging, she offered to share her spoils with me. Sometimes, upon noticing I'd come home empty-handed, she quietly slipped into my fingers one of the plastic crown-shaped pins she had earned, meant to represent the crowns we would one day receive in heaven for memorizing so many Bible verses. It frightened me how much she looked up to me, how much she trusted me and rooted for me when I didn't deserve it. I was a good big sister to her until I hit puberty and in the ensuing existential crisis grew resentful of how effortlessly she was loved. Once, when I felt she had not been adequately blamed for some mishap we'd found ourselves in at home, I called her a goody-two-shoes and mocked her by singing the hymn "Holy, Holy, Holy" with derisive jeer. It is the cruelest thing I have ever done to anyone. Ever. Hers was such a tender spirit that I knew instantly I had bruised something precious, just for the sport of it, and that I was capable of greater evil than I'd ever imagined. Not even the waters of baptism could wash that sin away, I was sure of it.

On our baptism day, we followed my mother into the sanctuary's stark bridal room where we pulled thin baptismal robes over T-shirts and jean shorts. I felt anxious about my breasts. My "stumbling blocks" had emerged early and generously, and I felt like the Whore of Babylon every time I caught a Sunday school classmate's eye on them. (I didn't learn to deconstruct modesty culture until after college, and by then it was too late.) Wet clothes would do me no favors, this much I knew. Fortunately, we were supposed to cross our arms in front of us before getting dunked anyway, and Mom had layered me up with a training bra, undershirt, and thick cotton tee. She ran a brush through my limp brown hair that hung like a mop strings beneath a tangle of artificially poofed bangs, and I watched her brown eyes scan the eczema breaking out on my arms, my stooped shoulders, the gap between my teeth. I refused to wear makeup, and it drove her crazy, especially on a day when any trace of color in my pallid face got washed out by a white robe. Amanda, of course, looked angelic with her hair curled and pulled into bouncy, asymmetrical pigtails—a Precious Moments figurine standing next to a frightened, busty ghost.

"Good news," Mom said, her cheeriness pronounced against the nervous tension. "I remembered to bring a hair dryer."

Well, that was a relief.

With my father overseeing my theological development, my poor mother was left to steer me through the social nuances of church life, a task I made considerably more difficult for her by taking the former far more seriously than the latter. It's one thing to explain to an eleven-year-old that there's no way to know if Anne Frank went to heaven or hell, quite another to explain why such a question might have been an inappropriate one to pose at a bridal shower in front of the church ladies. But such was the nature of my small talk. Had I inherited more of my mother's beauty and charm or shared some of my sister's virtue, I might have gotten away with it, but instead I struggled through the trappings of Southern religious culture where a good Christian girl is expected to at least talk about the weather or football before getting to eternal damnation. A lifelong introvert, I never mastered the art of the schmooze. In addition, I purposefully defied my mother by refusing to wear lipstick or carry a purse or care much at all about what I wore to church, precisely because I knew these things were important to her. I liked to think of myself as a tomboy (like my hero Laura Ingalls Wilder), but without the interest in competitive sports or the outdoors. Fortunately, my mother has a weakness for rooting for the underdog, and so I never doubted she was rooting for me.

I remember very little from the baptism service, except that the sanctuary looked so different from high up in the baptistery, like I was looking at it through a wide-angle lens. And I remember how comforting it was to wade out into the lukewarm water and meet my father there, familiar arms guiding me in, familiar hands clinching tight my nose, a familiar voice saying something about the Father, Son, and Holy Spirit, a familiar force pushing me down and pulling me back up again, like when he swung me in his arms. And I remember how I was glad to see my mother waiting with open arms to wrap me in a towel, and how we watched together as Amanda took her turn and waded in, the water so much deeper around her little shoulders. There was a reception after, and someone had thought to make deviled eggs because they knew they were my favorite.

But most of all, I remember wondering why I didn't feel cleaner, why I didn't feel holier or lighter or closer to God when I'd just been born again . . . *again.* I wondered if perhaps my Pentecostal classmates were right and I needed a second baptism of the Holy Spirit, or if I had not been solemn enough or prepared enough for the baptism to work. I hadn't yet learned that you tend to come out of the big moments—the wedding, the book deal, the trip, the death, the birth—as the exact same person who went in, and that perhaps the strangest surprise of life is it keeps on happening to the same ol' *you.*

It is said that when Martin Luther would slip into one of his darker places (which happened a lot, the dude was totally bipolar), he would comfort himself by saying, "Martin, be calm, you are baptized." I suspect his comfort came not from recalling the moment of baptism itself, or in relying on baptism as a sort of magic charm, but in remembering what his baptism signified: his identity as a beloved child of God. Because ultimately, baptism is a naming. When Jesus emerged from the waters of the Jordan, a voice from heaven declared, "This is my Son, whom I love; with him I am well pleased." Jesus did not begin to be loved at the moment of his baptism, nor did he cease to be loved when his baptism became a memory. Baptism simply named the reality of his existing and unending belovedness. As my friend Nadia puts it, "Identity. It's always God's first move."[9]

So, too, it is with us. In baptism, we are identified as beloved children of God, and our adoption into the sprawling, beautiful, dysfunctional family of the church is celebrated by whoever happens to be standing on the shoreline with a hair dryer and deviled eggs. This is why the baptism font is typically located near the entrance of a church. The central aisle represents the Christian's journey through life toward God, a journey that begins with baptism.

The good news is you are a beloved child of God; the bad news is you don't get to choose your siblings. Nadia is a Lutheran pastor who grew up in a fundamentalist Churches of Christ tradition that, like mine, prohibited women from becoming pastors. When she converted to Lutheranism, she asked her Lutheran mentor to rebaptize her. Her mentor wisely declined, reminding her that an act of God cannot be undone or redone. Though she had left the company and the ways of her first church, she couldn't blot them out of her spiritual genealogy. They were still her family.

Like Nadia, I've wrestled with the evangelical tradition in which I was raised, often ungracefully. At times I've tried to wring the waters of my first baptism out of my clothes, shake them out of my hair, and ask for a do-over in some other community where they ordain women, vote for Democrats, and believe in evolution. But Jesus has this odd habit of allowing ordinary, screwed-up people to introduce him, and so it was ordinary, screwed-up people who first told me I was a beloved child of God, who first called me a Christian. I don't know where my story of faith will take me, but it will always begin here. That much can never change.

I was baptized by my father. And by my mother. By Pastor

George, by my Sunday school teachers, by my sister, by that used car salesman who sang a sauntering gospel version of "The Old Rugged Cross" every Easter, by the boy who put boogers in my hair, by the little girl in the wheelchair who couldn't speak. I was baptized by Alabama, by Reaganomics, by evangelicalism, by Parkway Christian Academy, and Bible Chapel. I was baptized by Martin Luther King Jr. and George Wallace and Billy Graham. I was baptized by the sort of people who turn fish stories into sermons and listen to Rush Limbaugh and sometimes love me the wrong way. I was baptized by water and by spirit and by this strange bundle of atoms and genes and experiences God has assembled, delighted in, and in an act of absurd mercy named *Beloved*.

THREE

Naked on Easter

How bold one gets when one is sure of being loved.

—Sigmund Freud

IN THE EARLY 1920S, ARCHEOLOGISTS EXPLORING THE desert ruins of Dura-Europos, a Roman border city in modern-day Syria, uncovered a series of crude frescoes on the walls of a Roman home. The frescoes surrounded a bathing pool and depicted several distinct scenes: a shepherd carrying a lamb on his shoulders, a woman at a well, two figures walking across the sea as their comrades watch from a ship, three women approaching a tomb. The archeologists had discovered the baptistery of what remains the oldest known church building in the world.

Nearly two thousand years earlier, on Easter morning just before the sun rose, flickering lamplight would have illuminated the drawings as new converts to Christianity kneeled, stark naked, in the water of the baptistery. One by one, the men separated from the women, each publicly affirmed the tenets of the faith and renounced Satan and his demons before being submerged three times in the cold water—in the name of the Father, the Son, and the Holy Spirit.

"Dost thou renounce Satan, and all his angels, and all his works, and all his services, and all his pride?" Orthodox priests ask adult converts to this day.

"I do," says the convert.

"Dost thou unite thyself unto Christ?"

"I do."

"Bow down also before him."

"I bow down before the Father, and the Son, and the Holy Spirit."

After baptism, converts were given white robes to signify their new life in Christ and anointed with oil, marking them as members of the royal priesthood. They then joined their fellow believers to celebrate the eucharistic meal for the first time. The process was repeated every year, after several days of fasting and at the culmination of the solemn Easter vigil.[10]

These days, most churches don't begin their Resurrection Sunday service with a bunch of wet, naked people renouncing Satan and his demons at six o'clock in the morning. Such an approach would draw far fewer visitors than elaborate passion plays or Easter egg hunts promising cash prizes. Yet historically, the Christian life began with the public acknowledgment of two uncomfortable realities—evil and death—and in baptism, the Christian makes the audacious claim that neither one gets the final word.

Now, I'm as uncomfortable as the next Honda-driving, NPR-listening, *New York Times*–reading progressive with the notion of exorcising demons. When I get to those stories in the New Testament, I'm inclined to take the sophisticated approach and assume the people who had demons cast out of them were healed of mental illness or epilepsy or something like that (which, when you think about it, simply requires exchanging one highly implausible story for another). But lately I've been wondering if this leaves something important out, something true about the shape and nature of evil, which, as Alexander Schmemann puts it, is not merely an absence of good but "the presence of dark and irrational power."[11]

Indeed, our sins—hate, fear, greed, jealousy, lust, materialism, pride—can at times take such distinct forms in our lives that we recognize them in the faces of the gargoyles and grotesques that guard our cathedral doors. And these sins join in a chorus—you might even say a legion—of voices locked in an ongoing battle with God to lay claim over our identity, to convince us we belong to them, that they have the right to name us. Where God calls the baptized *beloved*, demons call her *addict, slut, sinner, failure, fat, worthless, faker, screwup*. Where God calls her *child*, the demons beckon with *rich, powerful, pretty, important, religious, esteemed, accomplished, right*. It is no coincidence that when Satan tempted Jesus after his baptism, he began his entreaties with, "*If* you are the Son of God . . ." We all long for someone to tell us who we are. The great struggle of the Christian life is to take God's name for us, to believe we are beloved and to believe that is enough.

Whether they come from within us or outside us, whether they represent distinct personalities or the sins and systems that compete for our allegiance, demons are as real as the competing identities that seek to possess us. But rather than casting them out of our churches, we tend to invite them in, where they tell us we'll be children of God *when . . .*

we beat the addiction.

we sign the doctrinal statement.

we help with the children's ministry.

we get our act together.

we tithe.

we play by the rules.

we believe without doubt.

we are married.

we are straight.

we are religious.

we are good.

But "the first act of the Christian life," says Schmemann, "is a renunciation, a challenge." In baptism, the Christian stands naked and unashamed before all these demons—all these impulses and temptations, sins and failures, empty sales pitches and screwy labels—and says, "I am a beloved child of God and I renounce anything or anyone who says otherwise."[12] In some Orthodox traditions, the convert literally spits in the face of evil before going under the water.

It's a brave, defiant thing to do. And Christians ought to do it more often, if not in our baptisms, then in our remembrance of them. Or maybe every time we take a shower.

In addition to proclaiming God's power over principalities, the oldest baptism rites declared God's power over death. Many of the first baptismal fonts were shaped as coffins, and baptisms took place just before sunrise on Easter morning to recall Christ's triumph over the grave. The Christian's descent into the water represents a surrender, a death, to the old way of living. Emergence represents a resurrection, a starting over again.

"Don't you know that all of us who were baptized into Christ Jesus were baptized into his death?" the apostle Paul wrote the Romans. "We were therefore buried with him through baptism into death in order that, just as Christ was raised from the dead through the glory of the Father, we too may live a new life" (Romans 6:3–4). Cyril of Jerusalem told the newly baptized that "by this action, you died and you were born, and for you the saving water was at once a grave and the womb of a mother." Luther described baptism as the drowning of the old, sinful self which he notes "is a mighty good swimmer," and Argentinian preacher Juan Carlos Ortiz has been known to use a startling baptismal formula: "I kill you in the name of the Father, and of the Son, and of the Holy Spirit, and I make you born into the kingdom of God to serve him and to please him."[13]

Death and resurrection. It's the impossibility around which every other impossibility of the Christian faith orbits. Baptism declares that God is in the business of bringing dead things back to life, so if you want in on God's business, you better prepare to follow God to all the rock-bottom, scorched-earth, dead-on-arrival corners of this world—including those in your own heart—because that's where God works, that's where God gardens. Baptism reminds us that there's no ladder to holiness to climb, no self-improvement plan to follow. It's just death and resurrection, over and over again, day after day, as God reaches down into our deepest graves and with the same power that raised Jesus from the dead wrests us from our pride, our apathy, our fear, our prejudice, our anger, our hurt, and our despair. Most days I don't know which is harder for me to believe: that God reanimated the brain functions of a man three days dead, or that God can bring back to life all the beautiful things we have killed. Both seem pretty unlikely to me.

Everyone's got an opinion these days about why people are leaving the church. Some wish to solve the problem by making Christianity a little more palatable—you know, cut out all this weird, mystical stuff about sin, demons, and death and resurrection, and replace it with self-help books or politics or fancy theological systems or hip coffee shops. But sometimes I think what the church needs most is to recover some of its weird. There's no sense in sending her through the makeover montage of the chick flick when she'll always be the strange, awkward girl who only gets invited to prom on a dare.

In the ritual of baptism, our ancestors acted out the bizarre truth of the Christian identity: We are people who stand totally exposed before evil and death and declare them powerless against love.

There's nothing normal about that.

FOUR

Chubby Bunny

It must be wonderful to be seventeen, and to know everything.

—Arthur C. Clarke

I WENT TO SCHOOL THE DAY AFTER THE MASSACRE AT Columbine High School, even though most of my classmates skipped.

"It's the perfect witnessing opportunity," I told my mother on my way out the door to catch the bus. "Everyone's scared."

Rhea County High School in Dayton, Tennessee, was exactly 1,318 miles away from Columbine High School, where the day before, on April 20, 1999, Eric Harris and Dylan Klebold had pulled two assault rifles, ninety-nine explosives, and two shotguns from beneath their black trench coats to kill a dozen of their classmates and a teacher before committing suicide. I'd heard on the news that some of the victims had been asked if they believed in God before they got shot, so as the first blue light of morning glowed in the bus windows, I prayed God would give me the strength to affirm my faith in the event of a dreaded copycat scenario that had so many parents, students, and teachers worried that morning.

As a senior and president of the Bible Club, I felt it my duty to lead the revival I felt certain the tragedy would ignite among high school students across the country. I'd been gunning for a revival ever since I entered the public school system when we moved to Tennessee two years after my baptism, a plan made considerably more difficult by the fact that nearly everyone in Dayton—home to the famous Scopes Monkey Trial of 1925—already identified as Christian. There were prayers before each football game and Bible verses on every business marquee. McDonald's and Hardee's hosted rival gospel sings for old-timers on alternating Thursday nights, and later, a lone bronze statue of William Jennings Bryan, legendary defender of fundamentalism, would be erected to guard the courthouse lawn. We had to form a double circle around the flagpole for See You At the Pole because so many of us showed up to take a stand for Jesus. Revival found the Tennessee Valley long before I arrived and had settled in, like a fog.

Still, I went to school every day determined to transform all the Christians there into *evangelical* Christians and set them on fire for God. I psyched myself up in the morning with Christian music from DC Talk and Audio Adrenaline. I wrote "GOD IS AWESOME" with magic marker on a strip of red duct tape and plastered it across my JanSport backpack like a bumper sticker. I looked for ways to redirect conversations about Friday night's football game into discussions regarding Jesus Christ's atoning death for our sins. I debated evolution with my lab partner. And the day after the Columbine massacre I found myself competing with Julie Andrews and the cast of *The Sound of Music* (I should have known we'd watch movies all day) as I hissed to the cheerleader two seats in front of me, "Do you know where you would spend eternity if you died today?" Had I not been so utterly sincere, so genuinely devoted to the eternal well-being of my fellow human beings, I would have deserved the glare she sent back. But for the most part my classmates were patient with me, even kind. A few of them, mostly boys who I now suspect had vested interests on account of my "stumbling blocks," humored me and showed up at my locker in between classes to talk about the merits of faith and whether I planned to be at the homecoming dance Saturday night. There were exactly two self-avowed atheists in my graduating class, and I'm pleased to say I converted one of them.

Well, I brought one of them to youth group; it was Brian Ward who converted him. Brian Ward was such a popular youth pastor that teenagers from churches all over the county showed up to "the Planet" at Grace Bible Church on Wednesday nights to sit on the floor and listen to him play guitar and talk about Jesus. Brian was allergic to Christianese, so it never occurred to him to talk about his walk with the Lord or about how he felt led to do this or that because something was laid on his heart. A Georgia Bulldogs fan with a thick Atlanta accent, Brian wore weathered baseball caps and T-shirts, sang like Eddie Vedder, and cussed from time to time. We suspected he got into trouble with our parents a lot, which only elevated his mystique. When we teased Brian about losing his hair, he reminded us of an obscure story from the Bible in which God sent two female bears to maul forty-two youths who dared tease the prophet Elisha for his baldness. "Two female bears," he'd say. "It's in the Bible, I swear. Look it up."

It was Brian's idea to call our Wednesday night meetings the Planet and to move them from the church sanctuary to a downtown storefront so we wouldn't feel like we were going to church. It was his idea to include students in leadership, in the band, and in important decisions about the future of the youth group. He watched the same TV shows we watched and laughed at the same parts we laughed at. His wife, Carrie, was pretty, sweet, and sensible, and I knew their little house by the river as well as I knew the homes of my best friends.

Brian managed to make church appealing without resorting to the desperate, strained strategies of other area youth pastors who tried to make Christianity "relevant to the youth." He knew you couldn't string up a volleyball net, crank up some Christian rock music, and expect jocks and band nerds, Goths and cheerleaders, hicks and churchy kids to put aside their differences and enjoy one another in the spirit of Jesus, and he only barely masked his disdain for youth leaders desperate enough to try. Instead, he outfitted our downtown storefront with La-Z-Boy armchairs in one corner, a foosball table in the other, video games in a side room, a giant stage in the back, and basketball goals and a volleyball net in the parking lot, and we counted it a success to have seventy or so teenagers together in the same space for three hours each week, with or without any *Breakfast Club* moments. Brian had achieved the *raison d'être* of every teenager past, present, and future: he was cool without trying to be. We adored him.

Even the back-row boys liked Brian, though they pretended not to as they shoved their hands in their pockets during worship and picked at the carpet during the lesson. Brian went fishing and bowling with them, shared inside jokes with them, and many years later, would officiate their weddings. With all the time Brian spent ministering to the back-row boys, you'd think more of them would move closer to the front of the room during worship to join those of us who were on fire for God.

"It's not my job to change people," Brian told me when I pestered him about it, "just love people."

I figured this meant he was playing some sort of long game, working his way into their lives before recruiting them to the revival. It never occurred to me that there were probably times when Brian was just loving me too.

I remember very little about church outside of youth group from those days, except that on Sunday mornings I got to see the boys from the youth group in their nice collared shirts and they got to see me in skirts. (By then I'd dropped the Laura Ingalls Wilder act and put on some lipstick.) We sat together in the back four rows of the Grace Bible Church sanctuary—a windowless, domed building that from the outside looked like a planetarium. Grace Bible Church was the largest nondenominational Bible church in town and had recently emerged from the worship wars of the '90s with a few minor flesh wounds and a compromise that left our congregation of around two hundred singing from the hymnbook for part of the service and an overhead projector for the other. Our pastor was an old family friend who had attended seminary with my father. The two had gone to get their physical for the draft together, and though neither had their number called, they recalled the event like old war buddies. Pastor Doug was a more scholarly, exegetical preacher than Pastor George and was a St. Louis Cardinals baseball fan, of all things. Our bulletins included detailed outlines of his sermons, often with subheadings beginning with the same letter: Salvation, Sanctification, Significance. I filled out every blank space, sometimes guessing at the next point (Service!) while the back-row boys blew spitballs at my head.

Not a lot of kids go to youth group to mellow out their religiosity, but Brian's relational style helped temper my crusader complex. He saw I had a knack for teaching and leading in a church setting, and on more than one occasion invited me to give the lesson (a privilege unheard of for a young woman in that context). He also convinced me not to ruin the Super Bowl party with an altar call at halftime and to relax and enjoy my friends on all those bumpy, open-windowed van rides to concerts and youth retreats that left my hair in tangles and my mind flitting from one cute boy to the next.

One such trip brought me back to Alabama each year for a weekend service project at Camp Maxwell in Haleyville. Camp Maxwell hosted underprivileged kids during the summer, but every spring invited privileged kids from youth groups around the Southeast to pour concrete, dig up stumps, and rupture water mains for Jesus. All the girls bought new overalls for the occasion. In the evenings, we gathered in an open-air meetinghouse to worship, shiver, and listen to fire and brimstone sermons from men whose theology Brian gently corrected for us on the van ride home.

It was at these gatherings that the Grace Bible Church youth group came to collectively appreciate our own exceptionalism, which we set out to prove each year by taking home the coveted Flush Valve Award. The Flush Valve Award looked exactly as it sounds, like a toilet flush valve mounted to a slab of pinewood, and was awarded to whichever youth group accumulated the most points over the weekend for victories in sports, games, Bible quizzes, and the all-important talent show. Most of these activities were easy wins for the Grace Bible Church contingency on account of our diversity. We boasted musicians, athletes, Bible nerds, and drama geeks in equal measure. One year, we earned a standing ovation at the talent show when we pulled off a miniature production of Stomp, with members of the high school drum line hammering away at empty garbage cans.

Our weakness lay in the games department. Now understand, *games* in the context of a Christian youth group means something entirely different than the same word in any other context. I suspect that in the late '90s alone, youth group games were responsible for millions of mono breakouts, thousands of broken bones, dozens of stomach pumps, and countless hours of therapy, for they typically involved placing insecure, hormonally charged teenagers in as physically awkward and borderline dangerous a situation as possible, preferably in the company of food, in a misguided effort to "break the ice" that invariably resulted in someone either throwing up or getting an erection.

There were trust falls and relay races and high-stakes, high-speed versions of Duck-Duck-Goose, musical chairs, dodgeball, and (until it was banned because I think it actually killed some people) Red Rover. We played sardines (cram twenty-five youths into the same dark hiding space for an hour), Suck-and-Blow (pass the credit card around the circle using only the suction from your mouths), and Two-Buck Chuck (chug a half gallon of milk without throwing up and win two dollars). There was the one where you had to bob for Snickers bars in a toilet bowl filled with lemonade, the one where you had to eat a banana with a pair of panty hose over your head, and the one where you tossed cheese puffs at your partner's shaving cream–covered face. It was a perpetual circus of delight for us introverts, obviously.

I recently exchanged youth group war stories with some of my readers on Twitter, and their accounts were chilling:

> "I've seen people drink milkshakes made from happy
> meals."
> "I once saw peanut butter licked from a dude's armpit."
> "We took the smallest middle-schoolers and duct-
> taped them to the wall. The team whose person
> stayed on the wall the longest won."
> "Steal the bacon with petroleum jelly and watermelons.
> Three students with concussions and one youth
> leader with a nipple ring ripped out."
> "Three words: strobe light volleyball."

"I had to eat an onion like an apple once. I don't
    remember why."[14]

Lucky for the Grace Bible Church youth group, Brian
struggled with moderate anxiety and therefore hated youth
group games as much as we did, so our exposure to them came
primarily through youth events like the one at Camp Maxwell
where we watched in horror as otherwise normal teenagers
tried to pull gum off the bottom of a dirty tennis shoe with
their teeth.

On the chilly night in question, the game that stood
between the Grace Bible Church youth group and the Flush
Valve Award was, of course, Chubby Bunny. Chubby Bunny is
a game in which several "volunteers" cram as many marshmallows as they can into their mouths and attempt to say "chubby
bunny" without throwing up or choking to death. The person
who can do this with the most marshmallows in his or her
mouth wins the game.

Now, the youth group of Grace Bible Church hated Chubby
Bunny. We were too cool for Chubby Bunny. We saw right
through the insidious ruse that was Chubby Bunny. But we
needed someone to play Chubby Bunny on our behalf if we
were to successfully win the Flush Valve Award and put these
other youth groups in their place.

As the competition sent their delegates to the stage to the
sound of cheers, we sat quietly in our five rows of wooden pews,
moving sawdust around with our shoes.

"We need a volunteer from Grace Bible Church!" someone
with far too many rubber bracelets on his arm shouted into the
microphone.

Names were whispered. Eye contact was averted. Brian
looked as scared as the rest of us.

Then, from the back, came a steady, certain voice.

"I'll do it."

We all turned.

Mike was a back-row boy if there ever was one. Tall and redheaded, he had a smart mouth and daredevil spirit and tended to divide his time between detention and the ER. When Mike didn't like something, he let you know it, and Mike wasn't too fond of church or school or Camp Maxwell. However, his eyes always betrayed a soft twinkle and he had such a wry, on-point wit that even we Bible nerds liked him. I know I wasn't the only girl who enjoyed drawing a smile out of his stubborn lips, across that freckled face, that strong jaw, and those wide cheeks . . . cheeks *made* for Chubby Bunny.

Without another word, Mike strode down the aisle and took his place between a girl in baggy overalls from Birmingham and a terrified junior high kid from Huntsville. They made him wear a trash bag like a bib. He was our Katniss Everdeen, our volunteer for tribute. We won the Flush Valve Award for the third straight year.

So this is how a girl who went to school prepared to die for her faith ended up shrieking with delight as back-row Mike shoved marshmallows into his face in pursuit of the Flush Valve Award. I attribute any trace of social acumen in my life to Brian Ward and my days in the Grace Bible Church youth group. At a time when most of my peers were struggling to find an identity, I knew exactly who I was: the church girl, the girl who always had a place in her youth group family, the girl on fire for God. I'm not sure I can ever calculate the value of that community, that sense of belonging and of being loved.

It never even occurred to me that such a fire could be washed out.

FIVE

Enough

Most of us come to the church by a means
the church does not allow.

—Flannery O'Connor

I'VE NEVER MET ANYONE MORE EXCITED ABOUT HIS
baptism than Andrew.

"Just thirteen more days!" the nineteen-year-old sang, as
though he were counting down to a graduation day or a wedding. "You wanna come?"

"All the way from Tennessee?" I balked, passing him the
larger half of a brownie I'd just split for us. "It's a bit of a drive
to St. Louis."

We were sitting at a round foldout table in the deserted
basement of a Methodist church in Columbia, Missouri, skip-
ping out on the afternoon session of the conference we were
attending in favor of acting as the self-appointed food critics for
the pastry items left over from lunch. (If the Baptists have the
corner on homemade chili—which they do—then Methodists

have it on pastries. I've never encountered a Methodist lemon bar I didn't like.) We'd found each other after my presentation earlier that morning, when Andrew—a dimpled, sandy-haired college student and faithful reader of my blog—seized me in the auditorium with a giant bear hug and a fit of boyish laughter. "It's okay," I'd assured the perplexed onlookers. "We know each other from the *Internet*."

"I honestly never thought I'd get baptized," Andrew confessed as he studied his half of the brownie. "I didn't think I'd ever be good enough."

"What sort of church did you grow up in?" I asked.

In response, Andrew pulled out his smartphone, scrolled through his pictures for a moment, found what he was looking for, and then handed his phone to me. On the cracked screen was a picture of the editorial page of a church newsletter. As I zoomed in closer, I could see the article was about same-sex relationships, which the author described as sickening. To the left of the headline, a silver-haired man in a suit and tie looked back at me with eyes that looked familiar.

"That's my dad," Andrew said. "He's a pastor, and he published this right after I came out."

My heart sank. For every teenager like me who knew only love and acceptance growing up in church, there were teenagers like Andrew who felt like strangers in the pews, strangers even in their own homes.

The sixth of seven children, Andrew grew up in a small, fundamentalist Presbyterian church in the South where his father served as pastor. There was much Andrew loved about his tight-knit faith community—its emphasis on Scripture, its commitment to evangelism, its familylike atmosphere—but as Andrew approached his teenage years, he found himself at odds with some of the church's more legalistic teachings, particularly his father's ban on contemporary Christian music and insistence that only the King James version of the Bible be used in church and in study. While his father emphasized reverence, righteousness, and self-control, Andrew had always displayed a tender, open spirit and an emotional connection to God. He scribbled endlessly in his prayer journal during his father's sermons, conversing with God as with a close friend. Though he occasionally rebelled (the first time Andrew saw a movie in a theater, he was eighteen years old, and he snuck out with friends to catch *The Hunger Games*), Andrew loved Jesus deeply, passionately.

Which made his secret all the heavier.

About the time his friends started talking about girls, Andrew started noticing boys. Having been raised to believe that sexual orientation was a choice and that same-sex relationships were an abomination, Andrew feared his impulses were a result of sin, sin he begged God to purge him of night after night and day after day.

A 2012 entry from Andrew's prayer journal reads:

I'm so scared. I don't want to be an outcast . . . Do you care what I'm going through, God? Why did you make me this way? What are you trying to teach me, God? I lift my hands to you. I'm in your hands . . . Give me faith! Please! I can't hold on much longer.

But no amount of prayer or Bible study or self-discipline could change Andrew's orientation. Finally, after struggling with bouts of depression and despair, Andrew came to terms with his sexuality. He left home to attend college in St. Louis and he found a new church that accepted him as he was. His new faith community even arranged for him to be baptized, an experience Andrew had longed for since childhood.

"I was always denied baptism and communion growing up," Andrew said. "My dad told me I wasn't manifesting enough fruits of the Spirit in my life. He wanted me to wait until I was good enough, holy enough."

Andrew formally came out to his family on the Thanksgiving break of his freshman year. It didn't go well. Now Andrew lives in his dorm room, cut off from his family and working to pay for his education on his own. The last time he spoke with his father, Andrew was told he was going to hell.

But Andrew wasn't alone during that difficult Thanksgiving break. A whole team of people from his new church had committed to pray for him for those four days. Andrew knew he had their support through every painful moment.

"No church is perfect," he said. "But they've been good to me."

That's when I understood why Andrew had invited me to his baptism. I was part of the only family he had. Andrew's adoption into God's family had been far more tumultuous and painful than my own, but he wanted me to be a part of it simply because I was among those who would not turn him away, simply because I loved him as he was. Sometimes the church must be a refuge even to its own refugees.

I wasn't able to make it to Andrew's baptism, but I prayed for him that day, and I watched the video the church made to mark the event. In his testimony before his baptism, Andrew said, "I put off baptism because I felt like I was in a state of sin, like I wasn't good enough or fit enough to be baptized. But then I realized that baptism is done at the beginning of your faith journey, not the middle or the end. You don't have to have everything together to be baptized . . . You just have to grasp God's grace. God's grace is enough."

SIX

Rivers

*There is a tendency for us to flee from the wild silence and
the wild dark, to pack up our gods and hunker down behind
city walls, to turn the gods into idols . . . And when we are
in the temples, then who will hear the voice crying in the
wilderness? Who will hear the reed shaken by the wind?*

—Chet Raymo

YOU CAN ALWAYS PICK OUT JOHN THE BAPTIST FROM A
lineup of saints.

Among the dour, robed patriarchs, he's the one with wild
eyes and tangled hair, ribs protruding through sun-browned
skin, hands cradling a cross-shaped staff or a scroll that reads,
"Repent, for the kingdom of heaven is at hand." Basically, he's
the guy you'd avoid bumping into in the Walmart parking lot.

The miracle child of Elizabeth and Zechariah, John likely
watched his father perform ritual cleansings as a temple priest
in first-century Jerusalem. Levitical law required Jews to cleanse
themselves from impurities contracted through things like

menstruation, skin disease, or contact with corpses, and many Jews made pilgrimages to the temple to be immersed in water in preparation for festivals and holy days. Friends and family probably expected John to follow in his father's footsteps and become a temple priest. But John didn't stay at the temple. John left the city for the countryside and abandoned the ceremonial bathing pools for free-flowing rivers.[15]

Subsisting on locusts and honey and calling people to a single, dramatic baptism to symbolize a reoriented heart, John embodied the prophet Isaiah's imagery of a voice crying in the wilderness, declaring God was on the move and everything was about to change. John knew this God-movement would not be confined to the temple, but that "every valley shall be filled, and every mountain and hill shall be made low, and the crooked shall be made straight, and the rough ways made smooth; and all flesh shall see the salvation of God" (Luke 3:5–6 NRSV).

"Prepare the way of the Lord," he told the people, "make his paths straight" (Mark 1:3 NRSV).

The people didn't have to go to God anymore; God was coming to the people. And God, in God's relentless love, would allow no mountain or hill—no ideology or ritual or require-ment or law—to obstruct the way. Temples could not contain a God who flattens mountains, or ceremonial baths a God who flows through rivers. Repentance, then, meant reorienting one's life around this reality. It meant repenting of the old ways of obstruction and joining in the great paving of the path, in the demolishing of every man-made impediment between God and God's people, and in the celebrating of God's wild, uninhib-ited presence filling every corner of the earth. It meant getting baptized in rivers and getting out of God's way. After all, with enough faith, a person can move a mountain . . . even a moun-tain of her own making.

"The kingdom isn't *up there*; it's *right here*," John said. "Repent, for the kingdom is at hand. Prepare the way of the Lord. Make his paths straight."

I wonder if these words ran through Philip's mind when he baptized one of the first gentile converts to Christianity: an Ethiopian eunuch.

As the story goes, after Jesus had risen from the dead and instructed his disciples to go and practice resurrection in the world, the evangelist Philip was sent by the Holy Spirit to the "wilderness road" from Jerusalem to Gaza. There Philip encountered a royal eunuch from the distant land of Ethiopia who was reading Hebrew Scripture from the back of his chariot (Acts 8:26–40).

As a eunuch, this man would have been strictly prohibited from even entering temple grounds, much less participating in its rituals (Leviticus 21:20; Deuteronomy 23:1). He was a sexual and ethnic minority, and as such would have been totally excluded from the religious community in Jerusalem, even if he believed in Israel's God. Had he approached the temple for baptism, he would have been turned away.

Yet this religious outcast, this man who was thought to be in a state of perpetual uncleanliness, had gotten his hands on a sacred scroll and found a passage from the prophet Isaiah that resonated profoundly with his own experience:

> *He was led like a sheep to the slaughter,*
> *and as a lamb before its shearer is silent,*
> *so he did not open his mouth.*
> *In his humiliation he was deprived of justice.*
> *Who can speak of his descendants?*
> *For his life was taken from the earth.*
>
> ACTS 8:32–33

When Philip heard the eunuch reading these words aloud, he approached the chariot and asked if the eunuch understood them.

"How can I unless someone guides me?" the eunuch replied.

Philip climbed into the chariot, and as it rumbled through the wilderness, told the eunuch about Jesus—about how when God became one of us, God suffered too.

Overcome, the eunuch looked out at the rugged landscape that surrounded them and shouted, "Look, here is water! What is to prevent me from being baptized?"

We don't know how long that question, brimming with such childlike joy it wrenches the heart, hung vulnerable as a drop of water in the desert air. At another time in his life, Philip might have pointed to the eunuch's ethnicity, or his anatomy, or his inability to gain access to the ceremonial baths that made a person clean. But instead, with no additional conversation between the travelers, the chariot lumbered to a halt and Philip baptized the eunuch in the first body of water the two could find. It might have been a river, or it might have been a puddle in the road.

Philip got out of God's way. He remembered that what makes the gospel offensive isn't who it keeps out, but who it lets in. Nothing could prevent the eunuch from being baptized, for the mountains of obstruction had been plowed down, the rocky hills had been made smooth, and God had cleared a path. There was holy water everywhere.

Two thousand years later, John's call remains a wilderness call, a cry from the margins. Because we religious types are really good at building walls and retreating to temples. We're good at making mountains out of our ideologies, obstructions out of our theologies, and hills out of our screwed-up notions of who's in and who's out, who's worthy and who's unworthy. We're good at getting in the way. Perhaps we're afraid that if we move, God might use people and methods we don't approve of, that rules will be broken and theologies questioned. Perhaps we're afraid that if we get out of the way, this grace thing might get out of hand.

Well, guess what? It already has.

Grace got out of hand the moment the God of the universe hung on a Roman cross and with outstretched hands looked out upon those who had hung him there and declared, "Father, forgive them, for they know not what they do."

Grace has been out of hand for more than two thousand years now. We best get used to it.

And so the call persists: *Repent. Reorient. Prepare the way of the Lord. Make clear the path.* God's tumbling through the world like white water on rock. There's nothing left but to surrender.

PART II

Confession

SEVEN

Ash

As a father has compassion on his children, so the LORD
has compassion on those who fear him; for he knows
how we are formed, he remembers that we are dust.

—Psalm 103:13–14

WE ARE MADE OF STARDUST, THE SCIENTISTS SAY—THE
iron in our blood, the calcium in our bones, and the chlorine
in our skin forged in the furnaces of ancient stars whose explosions scattered the elements across the galaxy. From the ashes
grew new stars, and around one of them, a system of planets
and asteroids and moons. A cluster of dust coalesced to form
the earth, and life emerged from the detritus of eight-billion-year-old deaths.

Ashes to ashes, dust to dust.

In the creation story of Genesis, God shaped man out of the
dust of the earth and animated him with divine breath. God
placed the man in a garden by a river and taught him to tend it.
When God saw that man needed a partner in this work, God

created woman and together the pair learned how to be alive: to plant and prune, to laugh and make love, to crack open sticky pomegranates and dig dirt out from under their fingernails, to recognize the distinct melodies of the birds and to walk with God in the cool of the day. They lived in the shade of the Tree of Life and were naked and unashamed.

But when life was not enough, when the man and woman wanted more, they sought wisdom in the garden's only forbidden tree—the Tree of Knowledge of Good and Evil. They thought its fruit would make them like God. But in their grasping and rebellion, in their independence and greed, they instead learned fear, anger, judgment, blame, envy, and shame. When God came to walk with them in the cool of the day, they hid in the brush, afraid. So God banished them from the garden, away from the Tree of Life, and they understood that they would die.

"By the sweat of your brow you will eat your food until you return to the ground, since from it you were taken," God told the man. "For dust you are and to dust you will return" (Genesis 3:19).

Ashes to ashes, dust to dust.

When the descendants of Adam warred against one another, armies burned the cities of their enemies to the ground. The sons of Adam and the daughters of Eve knew well the smell of ash, the bitter aftertaste of forbidden fruit. They knew, too, the difference between good and evil, yet they chose evil again and again in a violent quest to be like God. The gray residue of incinerated matter signified destruction, mortality, grief, and repentance. In the wake of tragedy or in the anticipation of judgment, our ancestors traded their finer clothes for coarse, colorless sackcloth and smeared their faces with the ashes of burned-up things. They ritualized their smallness, their dependency, their complicity.

"Put on sackcloth, my people, and roll in ashes," said the prophet Jeremiah, "mourn with bitter wailing as for an only son, for suddenly the destroyer will come upon us" (Jeremiah 6:26).

Ashes to ashes, dust to dust.

The Tree of Knowledge of Good and Evil didn't reveal every secret. Even the wisest found its fruit pulverulent. Solomon declared, "Everything is meaningless. All go to the same place; all come from dust, and to dust all return" (Ecclesiastes 3:19–20). When Job demanded an explanation for his suffering, God asked, "Where were you when I laid the earth's foundation? Tell me, if you understand" (38:4). Job retreated to a heap of ashes and cried, "Surely I spoke of things I did not understand, things too wonderful for me to know" (Job 42:3).

Ashes to ashes, dust to dust.

Once a year, on a Wednesday, we mix ashes with oil. We light candles and confess to one another and to God that we have sinned by what we have done and what we have left undone. We tell the truth. Then we smear the ashes on our foreheads and together acknowledge the single reality upon which every Catholic and Protestant, believer and atheist, scientist and mystic can agree: "Remember that you are dust and to dust you will return." It's the only thing we know for sure: we will die.

Ashes to ashes, dust to dust.

But a long time ago, a promise was made. A prophet called Isaiah said a messenger would come to proclaim good news to the poor and brokenhearted, "to bestow on them a crown of beauty instead of ashes, the oil of joy instead of mourning, and a garment of praise instead of a spirit of despair." Those who once repented in dust and ashes "will be called oaks of righteousness, a planting of the LORD for the display of his splendor" (Isaiah 61:3).

We could not become like God, so God became like us.

God showed us how to heal instead of kill, how to mend instead of destroy, how to love instead of hate, how to live instead of long for more. When we nailed God to a tree, God forgave. And when we buried God in the ground, God got up.

The apostle Paul struggled to explain the mystery: "The first man was of the dust of the earth," he said. "The second man is of heaven . . . just as we have borne the image of the earthly man, so shall we bear the image of the heavenly man" (1 Corinthians 15:47–49).

We are not spared death, but the power of death has been defeated. The grip of sin has been loosed. We are invited to share the victory, to follow the path of God back to life. We have become like seeds about to transform, Paul said. "What you sow does not come to life unless it dies" (1 Corinthians 15:36).

Life to death, death to life—like seeds, like soil, like stars.

No wonder Mary Magdalene mistook the risen Jesus for a gardener. A new Tree of Life has broken through the soil and is stretching up toward the sun.

EIGHT

Vote Yes On One

I threw stones at the stars, but the whole sky fell.

—Gregory Alan Isakov

"GREAT IS THY FAITHFULNESS, O GOD MY FATHER."

I intone the words with perfunctory detachment, my mind raging dully against the Papyrus font in which they are projected onto the wall. The electronic drums have settled into a sleepy 3/4 rhythm, but the congregation of Grace Bible Church sings louder than before, buoyed by the familiarity of an old, simple hymn. They want to take it slower than the designated beat, and the drummer—a senior in high school with a mass of curly brown hair hiding his eyes—will fight them through the first stanza before surrendering to the slow, steady drone of two hundred Christians perfectly content to take their sweet time singing through the "summer, and winter, and springtime, and harvest" of God's unchanging love.

By the time we get to the seasons part, I've already dropped out, my voice failing at the second line of the hymn: "There is no shadow of turning with thee."

No shadow of turning. *Wouldn't that be nice?*

I feel guilty because there is a breast cancer survivor to my right and a woman recently widowed two rows ahead, each of them singing with raised hands and closed eyes. Their faith hasn't come easy, I know, but I resent them for it. I've done everything right. I've memorized the Bible verses and observed my quiet time. I've studied the famous apologists and taken the right classes. There was no great personal tragedy to shake my foundations, no injustice or betrayal to justify my falling away—just a few pesky questions that unraveled my faith like twine and left me standing here unable to sing a song I know by heart, chilled by a shadow no one else can see.

My husband of five years, Dan, stands beside me, steady as a pier tethered to a drifting boat. Once we are home, we will crawl into bed together—both of us still dressed in our church clothes, but with our shoes kicked off—and he will listen as I mumble through my litany of grievances: the political jab during the announcements, the talk of hell, the simplistic interpretation of a complicated text, the violent and masculine theology, the seemingly shared assumption that the end times are upon us because we just elected a Democratic president with a foreign-sounding name. I glom onto these offenses, not because they are particularly grievous or even real, but because they give me reasons to hate going to church besides my own ugly doubt. They give me someone else to blame. Maybe it's time to call it quits, we will say. Maybe let's give it one more week.

There are recovery programs for people grieving the loss of a parent, sibling, or spouse. You can buy books on how to cope with the death of a beloved pet or work through the anguish of a miscarriage. We speak openly with one another about the bereavement that can accompany a layoff, a move, a diagnosis, or a dream deferred. But no one really teaches you how to grieve the loss of your faith. You're on your own for that.

For me, the trouble started when I began to suspect God was less concerned with saving people from hell than I was. After graduating from high school, I enrolled in the Christian liberal arts college where my father taught theology, and as expected, I sat in the front row of my biblical world view classes and chugged down Christian apologetics the way most college students ingurgitate cheap beer. And for the first two years, I was intoxicated with certainty. Every question met an easy, satisfying answer, and I swallowed those answers whole. I settled into the convivial pleasures of college life—pranking my roommates, debating theology over cold french fries in the cafeteria, lugging Norton anthologies all over campus like a good English major should. But then the twin towers fell, and a part of the world I'd thought little about came to occupy my TV screen each night while our country occupied its lands. As reports of collateral damage slid across the crawler, it occurred to me that the women and children killed in Iraq's civil war were mostly Muslims, not so much by choice, but by birth. They were Muslims because they were born in a predominantly Muslim country to Muslim parents, just as I was a Christian because I'd been born in a predominantly Christian country to Christian parents. Was I was supposed to believe the same suicide bomb that sent a terrorist to hell sent his victims to hell too? Because they weren't evangelical Christians like me? Because they were born at the wrong place and the wrong time? And did this fate await the majority of my fellow human beings, including the millions who had never even heard of Jesus to begin with?

It was a nondenominational university so I found no shortage of answers. The Arminians said God *couldn't* save the lost without sacrificing our free will; the Calvinists said God *wouldn't* save the lost because, well, God just didn't want to. The Pentecostals told wild stories about angels appearing to secluded jungle tribes to distribute the gospel on banana leaves. The sophomores quoted Karl Barth. Everyone agreed we all deserved hell anyway, so I best stop asking questions and show a little more gratitude.

My classmates seemed wholly unconcerned when I pointed out the fact that, based on what we'd been taught in Sunday school about salvation, the Jews killed in the gas chambers at Auschwitz went straight to hell after their murders, and the piles of left-behind eyeglasses and suitcases displayed at the Holocaust Museum represent hundreds of thousands of souls suffering unending torture at the hand of the very God to whom they had cried out for rescue. I waited for a reaction, only to be gently reminded that perhaps the dorm-wide pajama party wasn't the best time to talk about the Holocaust.

Those first few questions about hell sent me sliding down the proverbial slippery slope and before long, I found myself questioning everything I'd been taught about salvation, religious pluralism, biblical interpretation, politics, science, gender, and Christian theology. Evangelicalism gave me many gifts, but the ability to distinguish between foundational, orthodox beliefs and peripheral ones was not among them, so as I conducted this massive inventory of my faith, tearing every doctrine from the cupboard and turning each one over in my hand, the Nicene Creed was subjected to the same scrutiny as Young Earth creationism and Republican politics, for all had been presented to me as essential components to a biblical world view.

"You can believe the Bible or you can believe evolution," a favorite professor told the student body in chapel one morning, "but you can't believe both. You have to choose."

That recurring *choice*—between faith and science, Christianity and feminism, the Bible and historical criticism, doctrine and compassion—kept tripping me up like roots on a forest trail. I wanted to believe, of course, but I wanted to believe with my intellectual integrity and intuition intact, with both my head and heart fully engaged. The more I was asked to *choose*, the more fragmented and frayed my faith became, the more it stretched the gossamer of belief that held my world view together. And that's when the real doubt crept in, like an invasive species, like kudzu trellising the brain: *What if none of this is true? What if it's all one big lie?*

As with the death of someone dearly loved, I felt the absence of my faith most profoundly in those everyday moments when it used to be present—in church, in prayer, in the expansive blue of an autumn sky. I became a stranger to the busy, avuncular God who arranged parking spaces for my friends and took prayer requests for weather and election outcomes while leaving thirty thousand children to die each day from preventable disease. Instead I lay awake in my dorm room at night, begging an amorphous ghost of a deity to save me from my doubt and help me in my unbelief. Reading the Bible only made things worse, raising more questions, more problems to be solved. The words of the worship songs in chapel tasted like ash in my mouth. I felt my faith slipping away.

"You have wrapped yourself with a cloud," the author of Lamentations wrote of God, "so that no prayer can pass through" (Lamentations 3:44 esv).

While my parents had always welcomed questions and discussion, my friends and professors diagnosed the crisis of faith as a deliberate act of rebellion. After graduation, rumors of my purported apostasy circulated around town, and I found myself on the prayer request lists of churches I didn't even attend. My best friend wrote me a letter comparing my doubts to a drug habit and explained that she needed to distance herself from me for a while. I still have about a dozen gifted copies of *The Case for Christ* stored in my attic.

No one could believe that Rachel Held—once such a promising young evangelist—was losing faith. Their prescriptions rolled in:

"God's ways are higher than our ways. You need to stop
   asking questions and just trust him."
"There must be some sin in your life causing you to
   stumble. If you repent, your doubts will go away."
"You need to avoid reading anything besides the Bible.
   Those books of yours are leading you astray."
"You should come to my church."
"You should listen to Tim Keller."
"You need to check your pride, Rachel, and submit
   yourself to God."

(Oh, if I had a penny for every time I've been informed by an evangelical male that I have trouble with submission, I could plate the moon in copper!)

It became increasingly clear that my fellow Christians didn't want to listen to me, or grieve with me, or walk down this frightening road with me. They wanted to *fix* me. They wanted to wind me up like an old-fashioned toy and send me back to the fold with a painted smile on my face and tiny cymbals in my hands.

Looking back, I suspect their reactions had less to do with disdain for my doubt and more to do with fear of their own. As my mother tried to tell me a million times, they weren't rejecting me for being different, they were rejecting me for being familiar, for calling out all those quiet misgivings most Christians keep hidden in the dark corners of their hearts and would rather not name. But like most twenty-year-olds, I didn't listen to my mother and instead approached my doubt the same way I had approached my faith—evangelistically. Where I sensed a calm sea, I conjured a storm. Where I found people happily sailing along in their faith, I rocked the boat. Where peace flowed like a river, I came in like Poseidon. You get the idea.

I was so lonely in my questions and so desperate for companionship, I tried to force the people I loved to doubt along with me. I tried to *make* them understand. This proved massively annoying to those friends who preferred to enjoy their dinner and a movie without a side of existential crisis—so basically, everyone. I was reckless at times, and self-absorbed, and I'm still mending some relationships as a result.

Oh, how I missed Brian Ward. He and Carrie moved to Dallas, Texas, a few years after I graduated from high school to serve one of the largest youth groups in the country at a megachurch there. We kept in touch, and through our correspondence realized we were asking many of the same questions and raising much of the same hell, but in wildly different contexts. Brian sent me book recommendations by e-mail and I discovered N. T. Wright, Barbara Brown Taylor, Shane Claiborne, and Scot McKnight—unlikely sirens calling from another world in which Christians could doubt, Christians could accept evolution, Christians could have women pastors, Christians could oppose war. I read *Blue Like Jazz* and *A New Kind of Christian*. A faint light seeped through the cracks of my battered faith. I used the word *postmodern* a lot.

"You should come back to Dayton and start an emerging church," I prodded in an e-mail to Brian one day.

"Don't think it hasn't crossed my mind," he wrote back.

It wasn't much, but on the Sunday mornings when I just couldn't will myself out of bed and into the pews, I worked over those words like a rubbing stone in my pocket. Then I'd pull my covers over my head and mumble something about just not feeling up to it before falling back to sleep.

....

Nothing brings you back to church quite like settling down. I met Dan my freshman year of college when we found ourselves sitting across from one another in Dr. Jim Coffield's nine a.m. Psychology 101 class. (Truth: we "found ourselves" sitting across from one another because, over a period of two weeks, I inched my way a little closer to the handsome, six-foot-four New Jersey native, thinking he wouldn't notice my subtle migration to his side of the classroom. He did.)

Dan is the son of a former pastor, and his parents divorced when he was a teenager, which is about all you need to know to understand why Dan didn't get freaked out over a little religious turmoil. He moved through the world with the patient maturity of someone who'd already had his expectations adjusted, who already knew that faith was something you took a day at a time, not something you figured out at the start. We dated for four long but happy years, and in the autumn after my graduation we married at New Union Baptist Church, a local establishment that had a sanctuary big enough to house Dan's sprawling Jersey family and half the town of Dayton. Marrying Dan was the best decision I've ever made, and if it's God's only extra mercy to me in this life, then it will be enough.

After we secured jobs in Dayton (Dan as a tech guy at Bryan College, I as a reporter for the local paper), we returned to Grace Bible Church, where my parents and a smattering of high school and college friends still attended. The congregation was warm, engaged, and well educated. A phalanx of finely dressed children chased each other down the aisles after Sunday morning worship. These were the people who threw us our wedding shower, embroidered our hand towels, and loaned us their power tools. Their initials are stamped to the bottom of casserole dishes I still haven't returned, their handwriting scrawled across half of my recipe cards.

We were, as they say, "plugged in" to a church. To be plugged in to a church is to be wired into a highly choreographed, interconnected system of relationships, programs, and events that together produce a society complex enough to put on a decent Christmas pageant. One's function in the collective is determined by age, gender, and marital/procreative status. So as a young married woman with no children, my job was to host wedding and baby showers, co-lead a newlywed small group, make casseroles for potlucks, and inform people who had no business asking that Dan and I would start a family "in God's perfect time."

I have witnessed firsthand how such a network can perform miracles: a month's worth of dinners for the mom undergoing chemo, a driveway full of men ready to haul furniture the minute the moving van pulls in, twenty-four hours of prayer and rotating visits during a complicated surgery, fully stocked cupboards for widowers, and hours of free childcare for struggling parents. These are the quotidian signs and wonders of a living, breathing church, and they are powerful and important and real. But to a woman for whom the mere mention of a "ladies' tea" elicits a nervous sweat, sometimes being *plugged in* felt a bit like being *assimilated*. There were rules in this society, particularly for women, and I still hadn't learned my lesson about avoiding the topic of eternal damnation at baby showers,

showers that were now, inexplicably, under my care. I was better suited for leading a Bible study or theological discussion, but those things happened at the men's breakfasts (because, apparently, only men like theology and breakfast foods), so instead I constructed diaper cakes and mixed punch and listened to women exchange gruesome and detailed birth stories before turning to me to sing, "So, when can we expect a baby Evans?"

On Sunday nights, Dan and I met with a group of five or six young couples in our home to discuss a church-approved Christian marriage book. Though the book's teachings on traditional gender roles made me groan from time to time, it provided enough conversation starters for those of us who had been married for a grand total of three years to dispense our superior connubial wisdom upon those who had been married for a grand total of two. But the real fun happened after the discussion, when our closest friends stuck around to pop popcorn, play Texas Hold 'Em, debate politics, and discuss every imaginable topic until someone realized it was almost two a.m.

It was in these late hours that we formed some of the most important friendships of our lives, the kind that go beyond small talk and beyond theological discussions to raw, unedited truth telling. We confessed our deepest fears and greatest doubts. We speculated endlessly about our futures and shared in one another's joys and disappointments. We argued and apologized. We spewed hot chocolate across the kitchen in laughing fits and watched reruns of *Arrested Development*. This was our communion, our confession. This was the church that made our little three-bedroom-two-bathroom house grow spacious as a cathedral. In the company of these friends, questions and doubts were met with sympathy, not fear. No one felt the need to correct or understand or approve. We just listened, and it was sacred.

Even after most of our group graduated to one of the many groups for young families, several continued to show up on Sunday nights, long after the length of their marriages and size of their families disqualified them from the newlywed category. Once we finished the marriage book, we didn't bother to pick up a new one. We just baby-proofed the house so the kids could run around and invested in some nicer poker chips. I'm not sure we qualified as an official small group anymore, but on Sunday nights we had church.

Sunday mornings, on the other hand, weren't going so well. On Sunday mornings, my doubt came to church like a third member of the family, toddling along behind me with clenched fists and disheveled hair, throwing wild tantrums after every offhanded political joke or casual reference to hell. During the week I could pacify my doubt with books or work or reality TV, but on Sunday mornings, in the brand-new, contemporary-styled sanctuary of Grace Bible Church, doubt pulled up a chair and issued a running commentary.

"America is a Christian nation," said the man making the announcements.

Is it?

"Those who do not know Christ will be separated from God for eternity in hell," said Pastor Doug.

Will they?

"If the Bible is the inspired Word of God then we must accept this as historic fact."

Must we?

"God has called us to pave the parking lot."

Has he?

All the beliefs I struggled with during the week were taken for granted on Sunday morning, accepted as self-evident fact. This made my own misalignment all the more pronounced.

Around me, people nodded their heads and raised their hands and murmured "amen," while I raged internally at their confidence, their blithe acceptance of the very doctrines that kept me awake night after night. I was surrounded by the people who knew and loved me best in the world, and yet it was the loneliest hour of my week. I felt like an interloper, a fake.

We could never predict what moment in the service would trigger a full-blown crisis of faith. Once, it was the kids' choir singing "Nothing but the Blood" during special music.

"Surely I'm not the only one who thinks it's creepy to hear all those little voices singing about getting washed in the flow of someone's blood," I muttered as Dan and I escaped out the double doors.

Another time it was a prayer about God granting our troops victory over their enemies as they served him in Iraq.

"Don't you think the Iraqis are just as convinced God is on their side?" I whispered.

Sometimes it was just the way people chatted in the fellowship hall about "those liberals," as if feminists or Democrats or Methodists couldn't possibly be in their midst.

Often it was the assumption that women were unfit to speak from the pulpit or pass the collection plate on Sunday mornings, but were welcome to serve the men their key lime pie at the church picnic.

Oh, Dan got to hear all about it on the drive home . . . and at lunch . . . and into the afternoon . . . and after we'd clicked off the lamps on our bed stands at night. Sundays were growing difficult for him too.

One muggy summer morning, when we'd roused ourselves in enough time to pull into the church parking lot just a few minutes late, we noticed a half-dozen red, white, and blue lawn signs growing from the strip of grass between the highway and the freshly paved blacktop. They said "VOTE YES ON ONE" across the top and "Marriage = 1 Man + 1 Woman" across the bottom. In the middle was a stick-figure family holding hands.

I groaned.

It's no secret that the Tennessee state legislature has kept itself busy over the last decade producing mountains of wholly unnecessary legislation designed to protect what it considers to be Tennessee's most threatened demographic: white evangelical Christians. One proposed bill would have made practicing Islam a felony, punishable by fifteen years in prison. Another sought to ban middle school teachers from even mentioning gay relationships to their students. House Bill 368 (signed into law in 2012) encourages teachers in public schools to "present the scientific weaknesses" of evolution and climate change. In 2013, panicked rumors among legislators that renovations to the capitol building included the installation of a "Muslim foot bath" were assuaged when it was revealed that the fixture in question was, in fact, a mop sink.[16]

That particular summer, Tennessee lawmakers were busy amending the state constitution to include a ban on same-sex marriage. Churches and conservative organizations across the state had organized a campaign to remind voters that if they wanted to say no to gay marriage they needed to vote yes on proposition one and the Tennessee Marriage Protection Amendment. Nearly every church in town boasted several signs on their lawns, and now ours did too.

"We might as well hang a banner over the door that says 'No Gay People Allowed,'" I muttered.

I didn't have a lot of gay friends at the time. I hadn't met Andrew or my friends Justin, Jeffry, Matthew, and Kimberly. I hadn't yet reconnected with those high school classmates who, before they came out, got as far away from Rhea County as they could. I wasn't even sure what I thought about same-sex relationships at that point in my life, but I had no intention of voting yes on prop one because I didn't see why my religious concerns should have any bearing on whether my fellow citizens enjoyed the same rights and privileges as I did under the law. When you grow up just a few miles from 16th Street Baptist Church in Birmingham, and when you move to a town situated on the old Trail of Tears where a man was once prosecuted and fined for teaching evolution, you get a little sensitive about constitutional amendments designed to restrict rights rather than protect them. Sure, the Tennessee Marriage Protection Amendment sounded like a good idea to a lot of folks at the time, but how would it sound in twenty-five, fifty, or a hundred years? I just wasn't convinced we had this one right.

Of greater concern to me was the way these signs were sprouting up like weeds in every church lawn in the county. If Christians in East Tennessee wanted to send the message that gay and lesbian people would be uncomfortable and unwelcome in our churches, that their identity would be reduced to their sexual orientation and their personhood to a political threat, then we'd sure done a bang-up job of communicating it. We'd surrounded our churches with a bunch of stick-figured families who, with linked arms and vacuous smiles, guarded our houses of worship like centurions. If you wanted to get through, you had to know your place in the chain. You had to assimilate.

During the announcements, a man I didn't recognize invited us to attend a meeting that night to discuss the "radical homosexual agenda in America and how Christians should respond to it." He spat out the word *homosexual* the same way others spat out the words *liberal*, *feminist*, and *evolutionist*, and it occurred to me in that moment that maybe I wasn't the only one who brought an uninvited guest to church on Sunday morning. In a congregation that large, there was a good chance the very people this man considered a threat to our way of life weren't *out there*, but rather *in here*—perhaps visiting with family, perhaps squirming uncomfortably with the youth group in the back, perhaps singing with the worship band up front. How lonely they must feel, how paralyzed. Sitting there with my Bible in my hands, twisting its silk bookmark nervously between my fingers, I realized that just as I sat in church with my doubt, there were those sitting in church with their sexuality, their race, their gender, their depression, their addiction, their questions, their fears, their past, their infertility, their eating disorder, their diagnosis, their missed rent, their mess of a marriage, their sins, their shame—all the things that follow us to church on Sunday morning but we dare not name.

The words from Anne Sexton's poem "Protestant Easter" floated into my brain:

> *Jesus was on that Cross.*
> *After that they pounded nails into his hands.*
> *After that, well, after that,*
> *everyone wore hats . . .*[17]

And smiles. And masks. And brave fronts.

I didn't stop going to church after the Vote Yes On One campaign, but I stopped being present. I was too scared to speak up in support of LGBT people, so I ignored my conscience and let it go. I played my role as the good Christian girl and spared everyone the drama of an argument. But that decision—to remain silent—split me in two. It convinced me that I could never really be myself in church, that I had to check my heart and mind at the door. I regret that decision for a lot of reasons, but most of all because sometimes I think I would have gotten a fair hearing. Sometimes I think my church would have loved me through that disagreement if I'd only been bold enough to ask them to. Like a difficult marriage, my relationship with church buckled under the weight of years of silent assumptions. So I checked out—first in spirit, then in body. When our closest friends from Sunday night moved to California, our interest in the social events began to dwindle. After a few months, Dan and I began sleeping in on Sunday mornings.

It is perhaps no coincidence that I discovered blogging around the same time, and along with it, a whole community of people from across the world who smiled back at me from the tiny avatars in the comment section and bestowed upon me, like gifts wrapped in delicate paper, two very powerful words: *me too.* Turns out I wasn't the only one struggling with doubt. I wasn't the only one questioning my church's position on homosexuality and gender roles and a whole host of other issues. I wasn't the only one who felt lonely on Sunday mornings.

Of course, blogging about these things meant airing my unpopular opinions like red bras on a clothesline, which meant talk around town only amplified. I became a recurring topic of conversation in the Sunday school classes I didn't attend (or so I was told). Word got back to my parents that I'd been questioning biblical inerrancy on my blog. I received a Facebook message from a friend who had heard from someone, who'd heard from someone else, that I'd become a Buddhist.

"A Buddhist?" I wrote back. "Oh, I'm not disciplined enough to be Buddhist."

"Praying for you" is all I heard in response.

Now, Pastor Doug made space in our church for differences, for tension, for diversity, and for grace. He made space in his calendar for old and young, wealthy and poor, educated and uneducated. He made space for those who agreed with him and those who didn't. But Pastor Doug made no space for gossip. The man simply has no patience for it. When a prominent couple in the congregation announced their divorce and whispers about the details rushed through town like a flash flood, Pastor Doug stood before the congregation and, in a rare moment of blunt candor, gave us direct orders: "More praying. Less talking." As far as Dan and I were concerned, this made him a hero.

In keeping with his character, Pastor Doug invited us to his office one weekday morning to discuss, in person, our conspicuous departure. We made some mistakes in leaving our church, but perhaps the biggest was in trying to slip quietly out the back door. We thought we were doing everyone a favor by avoiding a potential conflict, but my pastor friends tell me this is a bit like breaking up with a guy by simply not returning his calls. After fifteen years, I owed my church a DTR.

Following some awkward small talk, Pastor Doug told us he missed us, but he understood that sometimes when people's faith changes, so must their church. We sat in the twin occasional chairs across from his desk, Dan drumming his fingers nervously on his knees while I stared at the carpet and tried not to cry. (Dan, by the way, had been working through these very same doubts for years, only with his trademark lack of fanfare.) Around us, bookshelves lined with commentaries and devotionals seemed to ballast the speckled ceiling. We'd done our marriage counseling in this office. I hid behind the door once, during one of those lock-ins when the youth group played sardines.

When Pastor Doug asked if there was anything specific he could address, we focused on the church's fourteen-point doctrinal statement, which required a signature for full membership in the church. It had been Dan's idea to start with something concrete, something on paper we could delineate and name. *Belief*, after all, is the language of evangelicalism. Not sacrament. Not spirit. Not liturgy. Not tradition. Not discipleship. *Belief*. We'd been taught all our lives that it was shared belief that kept us in this community of faith, so we just assumed difference in belief left us out of it.

This led to some discussion over what exactly is meant by "inerrant in the original writings," "judgment and everlasting punishment," and "the act of creation as related in the book of Genesis." I raised a few concerns about the church's policy on women in leadership, which Pastor Doug confirmed prevented women from pastoral leadership and preaching. We never talked about Vote Yes On One. We discussed our departure as we would the terms of a contract we could no longer sign.

When the sun came in sharp and gold through the blinds we knew it was time to go. I said something about just needing some space to sort things out. Dan said something about appreciating all the church had done for us through the years. Pastor Doug, with the twinkle of a tear in his eye, said we'd always be welcome in this church. *Always*.

As we walked in silence back to the car, I knew we wouldn't be back, at least not as regulars. Dan grasped my hand, and I felt his sadness too.

I have friends who struggled for years to disentangle themselves from abusive, authoritarian churches where they were publicly shamed for asking questions and thinking for themselves. I know of others who were kicked out for getting divorced or for being gay. Those are important stories to tell, but they are not mine. I have no serious injuries to report, no deep scars to reveal. I left a church of kind, generous people because I couldn't pretend to believe things I didn't believe anymore, because I knew that no matter how hard I tried, I could never be the stick-figured woman in the Vote Yes On

One sign standing guard in front of the doors. I didn't want to be.

We crossed the parking lot, which still smelled of fresh asphalt, and climbed into the safety of our car. As soon as the doors shut, I put my head in my hands and cried, startled to tears by the selfishness of my own thoughts:

Who will bring us casseroles when we have a baby?

NINE

Dirty Laundry

Churches should be the most honest place in town, not the happiest place in town.

—Walter Brueggermann

In many churches, the holiest hour of the week occurs not in the sanctuary on Sunday morning but in the basement on Tuesday night, when a mismatched group of CEOs and single moms, suburbanites and homeless veterans share in the communion of strong coffee and dry pastries and engage in the sacred act of telling one another the truth.

They admit their powerlessness and dependency. They conduct "searching and fearless inventories" of themselves. They confess to God, to themselves, and to one another the exact nature of their wrongs. They ask for help. And beneath the flickering of fluorescent lights, amidst tears and nervous coughs and the faint scent of cigarette smoke, they summon the courage to expose their darkness to the light: "My name is Jeremy, and I'm an alcoholic."

I've heard many recovering alcoholics say they've never found a church quite like Alcoholics Anonymous. They've never found a community of people so honest with one another about their pain, so united in their shared brokenness.

"The particular brand of love and loyalty that seemed to flow so easily [in recovery meetings] wasn't like anything I'd ever experienced, inside or outside of church," Heather Kopp says in her memoir about getting sober. "But how could this be? How could a bunch of addicts and alcoholics manage to succeed at creating the kind of intimate fellowship so many of my Christian groups had tried to achieve and failed? Many months would pass before I understood that people bond more deeply over shared brokenness than they do over shared beliefs."[18]

The other day I was asked in a radio interview why I'm still a Christian. Since I've never been shy about writing through my questions and doubts, the host wanted to know why I hang on to my faith in spite of them.

I talked about Jesus—his life, teachings, death, resurrection, and presence in my life and in the world. I talked about how faith is always a risk and how the story of Jesus is a story I'm willing to risk being wrong about. And then I said something that surprised me a little, even as the words left my mouth.

"I'm a Christian," I said, "because Christianity names and addresses sin. It acknowledges the reality that the evil we observe in the world is also present within ourselves. It tells the truth about the human condition—that we're not okay."

"Confess your sins to each other and pray for each other so that you may be healed," instructed James, the brother of Jesus (James 5:16). At its best, the church functions much like a recovery group, a safe place where a bunch of struggling, imperfect people come together to speak difficult truths to one another. Sometimes the truth is we have sinned as individuals. Sometimes the truth is we have sinned corporately, as a people. Sometimes the truth is we're hurting because of another person's sin or as a result of forces beyond our control. Sometimes the truth is we're just hurting, and we're not even sure why.

The practice of confession gives us the chance to admit to one another that we're not okay, and then to seek healing and reconciliation together, in community. No one has to go first. Instead, we take a deep breath and start together with the prayer of confession:

> *Most merciful God,*
> *we confess that we have sinned against you*
> *in thought, word, and deed,*
> *by what we have done,*
> *and by what we have left undone.*
> *We have not loved you with our whole heart;*
> *we have not loved our neighbors as ourselves.*
> *We are truly sorry and we humbly repent,*
> *For the sake of your Son Jesus Christ,*
> *have mercy on us and forgive us;*
> *that we may delight in your will,*
> *and walk in your ways,*
> *to the glory of your Name. Amen.*[19]

The Lutheran Confiteor makes it even more personal:

> *I confess to God Almighty,*
> *before the whole company of*
> *heaven and to you, my brothers*
> *and sisters, that I have sinned in*
> *thought, word, and deed by my*
> *fault, by my own fault, by my*

own most grievous fault;
wherefore I pray God Almighty
to have mercy on me, forgive
me all my sins, and bring me to
everlasting life. Amen.[20]

These brave prayers are just the start. Like the introductions at an AA meeting, they equalize us. They remind us that we all move through the world in the same state—broken and beloved—and that we're all in need of healing and grace. They embolden us to confess to one another not only our sins, but also our fears, our doubts, our questions, our injuries, and our pain. They give us permission to start telling one another the truth, and to believe that this strange way of living is the only way to set one another free.

So why do our churches feel more like country clubs than AA? Why do we mumble through rote confessions and then conjure plastic Barbie and Ken smiles as we turn to one another to pass the peace? What makes us exchange the regular pleasantries—"I'm fine! How are you?"—while mingling beneath a cross upon which hangs a beaten, nearly naked man, suffering publicly on our behalf?

I suspect this habit stems from the same impulse that told me I should drop a few pounds *before* joining the Y (so as not to embarrass myself in front of the fit people), the same impulse that kept my mother from hiring a housekeeper because she felt compelled to clean the bathroom *before* the Merry Maids arrived (so as not to expose to the world the abomination that is a hair-clogged shower drain), the same impulse that Nadia refers to as the "long and rich Christian tradition which in Latin is called 'totally faking it.'"[21]

The truth is, we think church is for people living in

the "after" picture. We think church is for taking spiritual Instagrams and putting on our best performances. We think church is for the healthy, even though Jesus told us time and again he came to minister to the sick. We think church is for *good* people, not *resurrected* people.

So we fake it. We pretend we don't need help and we act like we aren't afraid, even though no decent AA meeting ever began with, "Hi, my name is Rachel, and I totally have my act together."

Dietrich Bonhoeffer observed this same phenomenon at the underground seminary he served during his protest of Nazi Germany:

> He who is alone with his sin is utterly alone. It may be that Christians, notwithstanding corporate worship, common prayer, and all their fellowship in service, may still be left to their loneliness. The final break-through to fellowship does not occur because, though they have fellowship with one another as believers and as devout people, they do not have fellowship as the undevout, as sinners. The pious fellowship permits no one to be a sinner. So everybody must conceal sin from himself and from the fellowship. We dare not be sinners. Many Christians are unthinkably horrified when a real sinner is suddenly discovered among the righteous. So we remain alone in our sin, living lies and hypocrisy. The fact is that we *are* sinners![22]

My mother used to tell me that we weren't the type of people to air our dirty laundry. What she meant was good Southern girls didn't go around talking about their troubles or divulging their secrets. (I can only assume it is by some divine corrective that her daughter turned out to be a blogger.) But this is a cultural idiom, not a Christian one. We Christians don't get to send our lives through the rinse cycle before showing up to church. We come as we are—no hiding, no acting, no fear. We come with our materialism, our pride, our petty grievances against our neighbors, our hypocritical disdain for those judgmental people in the church next door. We come with our fear of death, our desperation to be loved, our troubled marriages, our persistent doubts, our preoccupation with status and image. We come with our addictions—to substances, to work, to affirmation, to control, to food. We come with our differences, be they political, theological, racial, or socioeconomic. We come in search of sanctuary, a safe place to shed the masks and exhale. We come to air our dirty laundry before God and everybody because when we do it together we don't have to be afraid.

My friend Kathy Escobar spent many years climbing the leadership ladder at a megachurch in Denver before trading a life of religious success for what she calls a life of "downward mobility" inspired by the humility and poverty of Christ. As a counselor, Kathy had encountered Christians who kept their battles with pain and depression a secret from their churches, so she helped found and pastor the Refuge, an eclectic and growing faith community in Denver inspired by both the Beatitudes and the twelve steps of Alcoholics Anonymous.

Kathy discovered that when a church functions more like a recovery group than a religious organization, when it commits to practicing "honesty for the sake of restoration," all sorts of unexpected people show up.

"People who make $600 on mental health disability and never graduated from high school are hanging out with friends who have master's degrees and make $6,000," she said of the Refuge. "Suburban moms are building relationships with addicts. People from fundamentalist Christian backgrounds are engaging those with pagan backgrounds . . . Orphans, outcasts, prostitutes, pastors, single moms and dads, church burnouts, and everything in between are all muddled up together . . . It's wild."[23]

Kathy, who describes herself as a recovering perfectionist and control freak, doesn't glamorize the process. She admits the healing happens at a slow pace and that this much diversity often leads to awkwardness and drama. It's not exactly what you call a seeker-sensitive model—"most people don't go to church to get annoyed," the petite blonde says with a laugh—but through the Refuge she has experienced mercy, grace, love, and healing like never before. She says she'll never go back to the upward-mobility life again.

Rather than boasting a doctrinal statement, the Refuge extends an invitation:

The Refuge is a mission center and Christian community dedicated to helping hurting and hungry people find faith, hope, and dignity alongside each other.

We love to throw parties, tell stories, find hope, and practice the ways of Jesus as best we can.

We're all hurt or hungry in our own ways.

We're at different places on our journey but we share a guiding story, a sweeping epic drama called the Bible.

We find faith as we follow Jesus and share a willingness to honestly wrestle with God and our questions and doubts.

We find dignity as God's image-bearers and strive to call out that dignity in one another.

We all receive, we all give.

We are old, young, poor, rich, conservative,

liberal, single, married, gay, straight, evangelicals, progressives, overeducated, undereducated, certain, doubting, hurting, thriving.

Yet Christ's love binds our differences together in unity.

At The Refuge, everyone is safe, but no one is comfortable.[24]

Imagine if every church became a place where everyone is safe, but no one is comfortable. Imagine if every church became a place where we told one another the truth. We might just create sanctuary.

TEN

What We Have Done

... If what's loosed on earth will be loosed on high,
it's a hell of a heaven we must go to when we die.

—Josh Ritter

THREE HUNDRED YEARS AFTER JESUS DIED ON A ROMAN cross, the emperor Theodosius made Christianity the official religion of the Roman Empire. Christians, who had once been persecuted by the empire, *became* the empire, and those who had once denied the sword took up the sword against their neighbors. Pagan temples were destroyed, their patrons forced to convert to Christianity or die. Christians whose ancestors had been martyred in gladiatorial combat now attended the games, cheering on the bloodshed.

Lord, have mercy. Christ, have mercy.

On July 15, 1099, Christian crusaders lay siege to Jerusalem, then occupied by Fatimite Arabs. They found a breach in the wall and took the city. Declaring "God wills it!" they killed every defender in their path and dashed the bodies of helpless babies against rocks. When they came upon a synagogue where many of the city's Jews had taken refuge, they set fire to the building and burned the people inside alive. An eyewitness reported that at the Porch of Solomon, horses waded through blood.

Lord, have mercy. Christ, have mercy.

Through a series of centuries-long inquisitions that swept across Europe, hundreds of thousands of people, many of them women accused of witchcraft, were tortured by religious leaders charged with protecting the church from heresy. Their instruments of torture, designed to slowly inflict pain by dismembering and dislocating the body, earned nicknames like the Breast Ripper, the Head Crusher, and the Judas Chair. Many were inscribed with the phrase *Soli Deo Gloria*, "Glory be only to God."

Lord, have mercy. Christ, have mercy.

In a book entitled *On Jews and Their Lies*, reformer Martin Luther encouraged civic leaders to burn down Jewish synagogues, expel the Jewish people from their lands, and murder those who continued to practice their faith within Christian territory. "The rulers must act like a good physician who when gangrene has set in proceeds without mercy to cut, saw, and burn flesh, veins, bone, and marrow," he wrote. Luther's writings were later used by German officials as religious justification of the Holocaust.

Lord, have mercy. Christ, have mercy.

Likening their conquests to Joshua's defeat of Canaan, European Christians brought rape, violence, plunder, and enslavement to the New World, where hundreds of thousands of native people were enslaved or killed. It is said that a tribal chief from the island of Hispaniola was given the chance to convert to Christianity before being executed, but he responded that if heaven was where Christians went when they died, he would rather go to hell.

Lord, have mercy. Christ, have mercy.

After Puritans decimated the Pequot tribe in 1637, Captain John Underhill explained, "Sometimes the Scripture declareth women and children must perish with their parents . . . We have sufficient light from the Word of God for our proceedings."[25]

Lord, have mercy. Christ, have mercy.

In 1838, the United States government, under the leadership of Andrew Jackson, forcibly removed more than sixteen thousand Cherokee people from their homes in Tennessee, Alabama, North Carolina, and Georgia and relocated them to what is today Oklahoma. Thousands of Cherokee died of cold, hunger, and exhaustion on the journey West—on what is now known as the Trail of Tears—and even more perished as a result of their relocation. In his farewell address, Jackson declared, "Providence has showered on this favored land blessings without number, and has chosen you as guardians of freedom . . . May He who holds in His hands the destinies of nations make you worthy of the favors He has bestowed."

Lord, have mercy. Christ, have mercy.

In the years preceding the Civil War in America, Christian ministers wrote nearly half of all defenses of slavery. Methodist pastor J. W. Ticker told a Confederate audience in 1862, "Your cause is the cause of God, the cause of Christ, of humanity. It is a conflict of truth with error—of the Bible with Northern infidelity—of pure Christianity with Northern fanaticism."[26] Divisions over the morality of slavery split Baptist and Methodist denominations in America in two.

Lord, have mercy. Christ, have mercy.

On the second day of Martin Luther King Jr.'s imprisonment in a Birmingham jail, a guard slipped him a copy of the morning paper. By the dim light of his cell, King read the tall black letters that headlined the second page: WHITE

CLERGYMEN URGE LOCAL NEGROES TO WITHDRAW FROM DEMONSTRATIONS. It was the Saturday before Easter, the same day Jesus lay buried in the grave.

Lord, have mercy. Christ, have mercy.

In 1982, the president of Bob Jones University defended the Christian college's policy banning interracial dating, telling a reporter that "the Bible clearly teaches, starting in the tenth chapter of Genesis and going all the way through . . . [about] the differences God has put among people on the earth to keep the earth divided."[27] When the Supreme Court ruled against the university's tax exempt status, the administration at Bob Jones refused to reverse their policy and instead paid a million dollars in back taxes. The policy remained unchanged until the year 2000.

Lord, have mercy. Christ, have mercy.

In 2013, Uganda's parliament passed a bill criminalizing homosexuality with the sentence of life imprisonment. The lawmaker behind the bill, David Bahati, told media, "Because we are a God-fearing nation, we value life in a holistic way. It is because of those values that members of parliament passed this bill . . ."[28] The legislation is said to have been influenced by evangelical Christian missionaries to Africa.

Lord, have mercy. Christ, have mercy.

. . . .

For Ambrose, who defied the empire by blocking the door of his church until Emperor Theodosius had repented of his violence, *we give thanks.*

For the desert fathers and mothers who fled the violence and excess of the empire to inspire generations to live more simply and deliberately, *we give thanks.*

For John Huss, who spoke out against the church's sale of indulgences, protested the Crusades, and was burned at the stake for obeying his conscience, *we give thanks.*

For Teresa of Avila, who overcame opposition from the aristocracy and the church to advance sweeping monastic reforms, *we give thanks.*

For Pedro Claver, the Jesuit priest who devoted his life to serving the black slaves of Colombia, especially those suffering from leprosy and smallpox brought by their conquerors, *we give thanks.*

For Anne Hutchinson, who knew it was illegal for women to teach from the Bible in the Massachusetts Bay Colony, but did it anyway, *we give thanks.*

For William Wilberforce, who channeled his evangelical fervor into abolishing slavery in the British Empire, vowing "never, never will we desist till we have wiped away this scandal from the Christian name,"[29] *we give thanks.*

For Sojourner Truth, who proclaimed her own humanity in a culture that did not recognize it, *we give thanks.*

For Maximilian Kolbe, the Franciscan friar who volunteered to die in the place of a Jewish stranger at Auschwitz, *we give thanks.*

For the pastors, black and white, who linked arms with Martin Luther King Jr. and marched on Washington, *we give thanks.*

For Rosa Parks, who kept her seat, *we give thanks.*

For all who did the right thing even when it was hard, *we give thanks.*

....

Restore us, good Lord, and let your anger depart from us;
Favorably hear us, for your mercy is great.
Accomplish in us the work of your salvation,
That we may show forth your glory in the world.
By the cross and passion of your Son our Lord,
Bring us with all your saints to the joy of his resurrection.[30]

ELEVEN

Meet the Press

Scratch any cynic and you will find a disappointed idealist.

—George Carlin

For the first few months after leaving church, Dan and I spent Sunday mornings doing exactly what we'd been told all the other heathens did on the first day of the week: sleeping in, making pancakes, and sipping our specialty dark roast coffee while watching *Meet the Press* in our pajamas. We were one *New York Times* crossword puzzle away from liberal nirvana, and it was wonderful.

I've known many Christians who say they had to leave the church to discover Sabbath. Indeed, unplugging from a church can have the same effect as unplugging from the Internet or a demanding job. Suddenly the days seem longer, fuller, and more saturated with color. It's like climbing out of a too-small space and drinking in fresh air again, or like rolling down the windows on an open road and letting the wind wreck your hair. You go on hikes and explore new spiritual practices involving prayer beads and meditation. You talk about how the oaks are your cathedral, the honeysuckles your incense, and the river over the rocks your hymn. You entertain the idea of taking up a new hobby—origami, perhaps, or yoga—and start writing poetry again. This lasts for a good three weeks until one morning you decide to try an episode of *Battlestar Galactica* on Netflix and the next thing you know, it's dinnertime and you still haven't put on a bra. Things can devolve rather quickly.

At first, in an effort to keep our truancy out of the prayer chain, I'd throw on a skirt and heels before heading to the grocery store on Sunday, just in case I bumped into someone from Grace Bible Church and needed to appear like I'd come from some other imaginary church we were attending. Folks get concerned when you leave their church; they get downright judgey when you don't bother to pick out a new one. Behind all the starched smiles and polite questions I saw the same prejudices I'd once nursed against the unchurched, people I'd assumed were too lazy, preoccupied, and self-centered to bother with God. Eventually, I learned to do my shopping between ten and eleven a.m., right in the middle of church hour, when spotting a familiar face in the checkout line is like catching someone with their eyes open during prayer. You're both busted.

By this time, traffic to the blog had picked up, so when I worked up the nerve to write about leaving church, a lot of people wrote back:

> "I recently left a congregation too . . . The culminating factor for me was when I was told I could no longer serve in our hot meal and food delivery ministry which feeds the homeless and poor in our community because I wrote a letter to the editor of the newspaper supporting marriage equality."—Leslie

"I still go because my family likes the fellowship, but mentally I left years ago. The reasons I checked out were: the use of fear to motivate people into action and keep them in line; doubts were not discussed . . . no one shared their own personal struggles, and if someone ever did, they became the hot topic of church gossip; I would have more doubts that God existed after listening to the sermon than before."—Rick

"I left church because I was taught from a very young age that I was an abomination and should be put to death. I tried to kill myself twice as a teen because I felt God would not love or accept me as I was born."—Tim

"I left because I got sick of hearing, 'What part of your walk is not right with God?' because I suffer from a chronic illness."—Beth

"We left for so many reasons, but the night we made the decision for good was the night my husband looked at our tiny newborn daughter sleeping in my arms and said, 'I don't want her to ever know that God, the God we grew up with, the one the church at large preaches. I don't want her to grow up with the crap we did. I want her to know God, but not that God. Never ever that God.'"—C. J.

"I left because I was repeatedly molested by a pulpit minister while an entire congregation looked the other way."—Kate

"The reason twentysomethings are leaving church is because of a consumer mentality. 'It's all about me.' 'I leave because I feel this way or that.' Church isn't about you! It's about worshipping Jesus . . . Instead of being consumers, let's go to church and ask what we can give Jesus because of all he has given us."—Dustin

"I've only seen one person in all the comments mention the reason we go to church: to glorify God . . . This is not an easy thing to hear because we are saturated in our Western culture and church with wanting things 'my way' when what really matters is that God gets his way."—Matthew

"We stay because of John, who prays for my family every single day . . . and the Smiths, who hosted my husband's high school group forty years ago and still pray for us . . . and Marilynne, who would slip me a five-dollar bill on Sunday because we are in ministry . . . and Brooks, who is developmentally disabled and loves to stand in the front, in the middle, and enjoy the signing . . . True, the rest of it drives me crazy, but where else would any of those things happen?"—Carolyn

"As a pastor, I go to church because I'm paid to be there. I'm scared to tell anyone that, deep down, I'm not sure I believe in God."—Anonymous

As I continued to engage in conversations like these, I came to see just how much tension and misunderstanding can exist between the churched and the unchurched, particularly when we are unfamiliar with one another's stories. It's easy for church folks to dismiss my entire generation as fickle consumers who bail on church the minute it gets hard, but what about the young woman who left her church because it protected her abusive husband and blamed her for their divorce? Is she just a product of a consumer culture? Should she be blamed for needing some time to recover from her experience? What about the family that left because their autistic child struggled with sensory overload during worship? Are they being too selfish, too demanding? And what about the college student who waits tables on Sunday mornings, or the couple who were told by their pastor that faulty parenting had made their kid gay, or the skeptic whose questions were met with platitudes, or the woman whose battle with depression just makes it too hard to get out of bed? The last thing these people need is one more person calling them failures, one more person piling on the guilt and shame.

Conversely, I noticed an assumption among many of the unchurched that those who remain in the pews do so as unthinking, uncritical drones just going through the motions to maintain their membership in the country club. I read snide comments about preserving power structures, keeping up with the Joneses, and ensuring that the pastor stays "fat and happy" with his coffers of tithe money. But for every story of exclusion, judgment, and even abuse, there are stories of inclusion, healing, and justice. We can't just dismiss the experience of the single mom for whom the church-hosted baby shower made all the difference. Or the Burmese refugee whose faith community helped her learn English and find employment when she was far from home. Or the pastor who spent more than a decade working within his denomination to enact changes in favor of gender equity.

Our reasons for staying, leaving, and returning to church are as complex and layered as we are. They don't fit in the boxes we check in the surveys or the hurried responses we deliver at dinner parties. How easy it is to judge when we don't know all the details. How easy it is to offer advice when what is needed is empathy. How easy it is to forget that, in the words of novelist Zadie Smith, "every person is a world."

"When I get honest," writes Brennan Manning, "I admit I am a bundle of paradoxes. I believe and I doubt, I hope and get discouraged, I love and I hate, I feel bad about feeling good, I feel guilty about not feeling guilty. I am trusting and suspicious. I am honest and I still play games. Aristotle said I am a rational animal; I say I am an angel with an incredible capacity for beer."[31]

And so, the same ganglia of impulses and intentions, hopes and frustrations that called me out of church followed me around when, after six months of *Battlestar Galactica* and *Meet the Press*, Dan and I decided to try church again.

We googled "Rhea County churches," and the resulting map appeared to have contracted a severe case of chicken pox. Hundreds of red dots marking churches of all sizes and denominations speckled the screen. The minute he saw it, Dan released a deep, resigned sigh and handed me the laptop, the prospect of testing each notch in the Bible Belt a bit too overwhelming for him to bear before his second cup of coffee. I assured him we could narrow the search by process of elimination, but even after we'd filtered out the Southern Baptists (too conservative), the Unitarians (too liberal), and the Jehovah's Witnesses (too . . . friendly), we still faced hundreds of options.

In a small Southern town there are typically just a few main players around which most of the faithful coalesce, so we began by visiting those, a move that kicked the local gossip into full gear on account of the fact that we drove the only turquoise 1994 Plymouth Acclaim in town, which, when spotted in the parking lot of the liquor store, doctor's office, or the First United Methodist Church, could start all sorts of wild rumors.

During Lent, we received ashes at St. Matthew's, a dwindling Episcopal congregation that met in a converted home rendering the "smells and bells" of the traditional liturgy a tad more awkward than awe-inspiring. On Good Friday, we cried "Crucify him!" with the Catholics at St. Bridget's, perhaps the most ethnically diverse congregation in town with its mix of sprawling Latino families and displaced Yankees, all gathered beneath an imposing crucifix. On Easter we went back to Grace, where everyone was a little too happy to see us. By Pentecost, we'd found our way to the same Methodist church where William Jennings Bryan made his last public appearance after the Scopes Trial and where the entire sanctuary was decorated like a carnival for vacation Bible school.[32]

"What'd you think?" Dan asked as we buckled into the Acclaim after another Sunday under the big top.

"I wonder if they realize their worship songs include both amillennial and premillennial theology," I said with a sigh. "Also, what's this business from the preacher about Moses writing Numbers? I mean, *everyone* knows Moses didn't actually write the book of Numbers. It originated from a combination of written and oral tradition and was assembled and edited by Jewish priests sometime during the postexilic period as an exercise in national self-definition. You can look that up on *Wikipedia*. And, while we're at it, a bit more Christology applied to the Old Testament text would be nice."

"Um, Rach, the sermon today was about *humility*."

Lord, have mercy.

See, I've got this coping mechanism thing where, when I'm feeling frightened or vulnerable or over my head, I intellectualize the situation to try and regain a sense of control. (I've read a lot of books on air travel, parenting, and death.) It was scary starting over at a new church and trying to make new friends, so before each visit, I girded myself with a sense of smug detachment wherein I could observe the proceedings from the safety of my intellectual superiority, certain I could do a better job at running the show thanks to my expertise as, you know, *a Christian blogger.* Oh, I talked a big game about the importance of ecumenicism and the beauty of diversity within the global church, but when I deigned to show up at one of these unsuspecting congregations, I sat in the pew with my arms crossed, mad at the Baptists for not being Methodist enough, the Methodists for not being Anglican enough, the Anglicans for not being evangelical enough, and the evangelicals for not being Catholic enough. I scrutinized the lyrics to every worship song, debated the content of every sermon. I rendered verdicts regarding the frequency of communion and the method of baptism. I checked the bulletins for typos. In some religious traditions, this particular coping mechanism is known as *pride.*

I confess I preened it. I scoffed at the idea of being taught or led. Deconstructing was so much safer than trusting, so much easier than letting people in. I knew exactly what type of Christian I didn't want to be, but I was too frightened, or too rebellious, or too wounded, to imagine what might be next. Like a garish conch shell, my cynicism protected me from disappointment, or so I believed, so I expected the worst and smirked when I found it. So many of our sins begin with fear—fear of disappointment, fear of rejection, fear of failure, fear of death, fear of obscurity. Cynicism may seem a mild transgression, but it is a patient predator that suffocates hope, slowly, over many years, like the honey mushroom which forces itself between the bark and sapwood of a tree and over decades is strangled to death. When it comes to church, I am well acquainted with cynicism.

But perhaps the most unsettling thing about a new church is the way the ghost of the old one haunts it. For better or worse, the faith of our youth informs our fears, our nostalgia, our reactions, and our suspicions. My ears perked like an anxious dog's upon hearing evangelical language from the pulpit. Words like *holiness*, *purity*, *biblical*, and *witness* will always ring a bit differently for me than they do for someone who grew up Orthodox or Pentecostal or humanist or Sikh. I measured every new experience by what I loved or hated about evangelicalism, which put all these good churches filled with good people in the rather awkward position of the rebound boyfriend. Were it not for Dan's gentle admonitions, they might never have gotten a word in edgewise.

Having failed to locate the First Post-Evangelical Church of Our Lady of Perpetual Deconstruction, we settled into something of a church-hopping rhythm wherein we visited more liturgical churches on holy days and more familiar, evangelical churches the rest of the time . . . and by the rest of the time, I mean maybe once a month. We weren't exactly regulars. It occurred to me one morning as we snuck out of yet another service to avoid yet another awkward coffee hour that somehow, after all those years on fire for God, I'd become a back-row girl. I'd become the type of person for whom I'd prayed for revival. Only now I wasn't even sure I believed in revival anymore.

. . . .

Amanda got married in October, on an unseasonably cold and blustery afternoon. She walked down the aisle of Grace Bible Church with a bouquet of orange and lavender flowers in her hands.

When we'd finally reached the end of the reception, after the rice had been thrown and all the out-of-town guests lingered to talk about old times and help my parents pile presents into the back of their van, I found Brian and Carrie Ward and collapsed into a chair at their table. The room was dimly lit with orange and lavender lanterns, the tables sprinkled with rose petals and baby's breath. Frank Sinatra and Etta James crooned from the PA. Brian, who had lost a little more hair since our youth group days, looked uncomfortable in his wedding clothes, but before long, he'd loosened his tie and I'd kicked off my heels and we were exchanging stories about the Planet and Camp Maxwell and Chubby Bunny and laughing so loud we drew a crowd of former youth group kids to the table like bugs to a humming light.

Brian was full of nervous excitement that night, his fingers drumming the table with fury. I knew him well enough to suspect he was sitting on a secret, some bit of exciting news that only Carrie's kind-but-pointed gaze was keeping under wraps.

When Dan arrived to the table to see what all the commotion was about, Brian couldn't keep quiet anymore. He slapped the table and made his announcement.

"We're moving back to Dayton to start a new church," he said, his eyes dancing like a child's in the candlelight. "And we're going to need a team. Y'all in?"

And that's how a bunch of church dropouts became pastors.

TWELVE

Dust

*Here is a trustworthy saying that deserves full
acceptance: Christ Jesus came into the world to
save sinners—of whom I am the worst.*

—1 Timothy 1:15

JESUS WAS NEVER POPULAR AMONG RELIGIOUS LEADERS.
The experts on Scripture and purveyors of the law followed the
radical rabbi around Judea with suspicion, hoping to trip him
up with a theological riddle or catch him in some juicy indis-
cretion. In one strange story from the gospel of John, a group of
Pharisees reacted to Jesus' healing of a paralytic by chastising
the overjoyed man for carrying his freshly retired mat on the
Sabbath. Talk about missing the point!

It seems those most likely to miss God's work in the world
are those most convinced they know exactly what to look for,
the ones who expect God to play by the rules.

Of particular concern to the religious elite was how Jesus
associated with sinners. He'd been spotted around town not only

in the company of the poor and sick, the outcast and unclean, but also with tax collectors and prostitutes—people brazen enough to economize their transgressions. Word had it he shared meals with them in their homes. Some even said he enjoyed himself.

Now, this wasn't simply the sort of colorful company writers and artists tend to romanticize—hookers, drunks, vagrants down on their luck. Jesus broke bread with tax collectors, too, men who exploited the poor and assisted the Roman Empire in its oppressive policies. (Replace *tax collector* with *lobbyist* or *Wall Street executive* and you get the idea.)

These were the people who wore their brokenness on the outside, people whose indiscretions were so *other*, so uncommon, their entire personhood was relegated to the category of sinner. They were the people the religious loved to hate, for they provided a convenient sorting mechanism for externalizing sin as something that exists *out there*, among *other* people with *other* problems making *other* mistakes. It's the oldest religious shortcut in the book: the easiest way to make oneself righteous is to make someone else a sinner.

Jesus knew all about this sin-sorting system, so when the religious leaders challenged him about the company he kept, he replied, "It is not the healthy who need a doctor, but the sick. I have not come to call the righteous, but sinners" (Mark 2:17). This momentarily assuaged the religious leaders, who, of course, counted themselves among the healthy.

It's tough to identify exactly what the first followers of Jesus had in common. The Gospels speak of Jews and Gentiles, soldiers and farmers, men and women, rich and poor, sick and well, religious and nonreligious. No two people interacted with Jesus in exactly the same way, and few engaged in lengthy theological discussions or made a direct profession of faith before dropping their fishing nets, water jars, crutches, and money purses to follow this man who promised forgiveness of sins and life everlasting. It certainly wasn't shared belief that brought them together. Nowhere do the Gospels speak of converts reciting the "sinner's prayer" or signing a doctrinal statement or pledging allegiance to a creed. One of the first Christian missionaries, known as the woman at the well, was a Samaritan who sparred with Jesus over the details of when and where the people of God should worship. She was joined by devout Jews, Gentiles, zealots, tax collectors, conservatives, liberals, widows, fishermen, wealthy benefactresses, and impoverished beggars.

It wasn't shared social status or ethnicity that brought Jesus' followers together either, nor was it total agreement on exactly who this Jesus character was—a prophet? the Messiah? the Son of God? No, if there is one thing that connected all these dissimilar people together it was a shared sense of need: a hunger, a thirst, a longing. It was the certainty that, when Jesus said he came for the sick, this meant Jesus came for *me*.

"Blessed are those who hunger and thirst for righteousness," Jesus said, "for they will be filled" (Matthew 5:6).

"Woe to you who are well fed now," Jesus said, "for you will go hungry" (Luke 6:25).

When Jesus said he came not for the righteous, but for the sinners, he meant he came for everyone. But only those who know they are sick can be healed. Only those who listen to the rumblings in their belly can be filled. Only those who recognize the extent of their wounds and their wounding can be made well.

In another story from the book of John, the religious leaders take into custody a woman caught in the act of adultery. Armed with a Bible verse that prescribes the death penalty to adulterers, the scribes and Pharisees bring the woman to Jesus, throw her at his feet, and pose a challenge.

"The Bible says we should stone this woman. What do *you* say?"

It was a test. The religious leaders wanted to see if this controversial rabbi would be tough on sin, so they found themselves a sinner to condemn. They picked a clear-cut transgression with clear-cut consequences and passed around the stones. *Surely Jesus would not be so foolish as to contradict God's Word. Surely he would not risk the integrity of his ministry to show mercy to a sinner.*

In response, Jesus does the strangest thing: he kneels in the dust and starts writing in it with his finger. All eyes divert from the trembling woman to the ground, all the accusatory shouts hush to curious whispers.

The text leaves the content of his message a mystery. Perhaps it was the name of the woman's equally guilty partner, or a list of the sins of her accusers. It may have been a reference to Jeremiah 17:3 which declares that the names of those who turn away from God will be written in dust. Or maybe it was a reminder that "for dust you are and to dust you will return."

When Jesus finally straightens up and shakes the dust off his hands, he looks at the religious leaders and says, "Let any of you who is without sin be the first to throw a stone at her."

The gospel tells us it was the oldest in the crowd who walked away first. The younger ones soon followed suit. Before long, all that was left was a scattering of stones and the mysterious words of Jesus getting carried off by the wind.

At least for a moment, the religious leaders got it: Jesus hung out with sinners because there were only sinners to hang out with.

"Where are they?" Jesus asks the woman after they have gone. "Has no one condemned you?"

"No, sir," she replies.

"Then neither do I condemn you. Go and sin no more."[33]

We tend to look down our noses at these ancient people with their religious codes regulating everything from the fibers in their clothing to the people they touched. But we have our own religious codes these days. We have our own scapegoats we cast from our communities and surround with Bible-wielding mobs. We have sins we delight in taking seriously, biblical instructions we interpret hyperliterally, issues we protect over-vigilantly because it helps us with our sorting system. It makes us feel righteous.

"Let's not forget that Jesus told the woman to go and sin no more," some like to say when they think the church is getting too soft on other people's sin.

To this I am always tempted to respond: *So how's that working out for you? The sinning no more thing? Because it's not going so well for me.*

I think it's safe to say we've missed the point when, of all the people in this account, we decide we're the most like Jesus. I think it's safe to say we've missed the point when we use his words to condemn and this story as a stone.

Billy Graham once said, "It is the Holy Spirit's job to convict, God's job to judge, and my job to love."

Perhaps it would be easier for us to love if it were our own sins we saw written in that dust and carried off by the wind.

PART III

Holy Orders

THIRTEEN

Hands

I remind you to fan into flame the gift of God, which
is in you through the laying on of my hands.

—2 Timothy 1:6

THERE IS POWER IN TOUCH—A CONNECTIVE ENERGY, A
bond. Sweethearts know it in the tender frisson of fingers inter-
twined, children in the touch of a mama's lips to a bandaged
knee, the grieving in the gentle pressure of steady hands on
heaving shoulders. From infancy, we ache for the warmth of
one another's skin. Jesus didn't have to touch the blind man's
eyes or the leper's sores, but he did. The Son of God healed with
his hands.

From its earliest days, the church blessed its sick and commissioned its leaders with the laying on of hands, a practice so
central to the Christian faith the writer of Hebrews likens it
to baptism and repentance (Acts 28:8; Hebrews 6:1–3). Those
called to the roles of pastor, deacon, bishop, or priest—named
holy orders in some traditions—begin their ministry with the

hands of God's people placed prayerfully upon their shoulders or on their heads.

"Fill her with grace and power, and make her a priest in your church," the Anglican bishop prays over a priest at her ordination ceremony, hands resting on her head in dedication. "Make her a faithful pastor, a patient teacher and a wise councilor."

There is something about that touch, that act of consecration, which turns a prayer into a pulse that ripples right down to the toes. Just as God comes to us through water and wine, God comes to us through touch, through the holy acts of holy hands.

The hands of a pastor will baptize babies, type out sermons, and draw crosses of ash over penitent brows. They will break bread, and pour wine, and shelter unwieldy Advent flames. They will grasp the speckled arms of the elderly, the sticky fingers of toddlers, the trembling hands of the sick, the lifeless palms of the dead. And they will rest upon the heads of others so called.

"Do not neglect your gift," the New Testaments instructs, "which was given you through prophecy when the body of elders laid their hands on you" (1 Timothy 4:14).

Ultimately, all are commissioned. All are called. All belong to the holy order of God's beloved. The hands that pass the peace can pass a meal to the man on the street. The hands that cup together to receive Christ in the bread will extend to receive Christ in the immigrant, the refugee, the lonely, or the sick. Hands plant, and uproot, and cook, and caress. They repair, and rewire, and change diapers, and dress wounds. Hands tickle giggling children and wipe away tears. Hands rub heaving bellies of big, ugly dogs. Hands sanctify all sorts of ordinary things and make them holy.

Through touch, God gave us the power to injure or to heal, to wage war or to wash feet. Let us not forget the gravity of that. Let us not forget the call.

FOURTEEN

The Mission

*Grace is not so poor a thing that it cannot
present itself in any number of ways.*

—Marilynne Robinson

April 2010

Our first Easter, we met in the apartment above the funeral
home. It's where we gathered every week, but on that holy evening, as the sun set on Resurrection Day, I was struck by the
poetry of it, so I lit the paschal candle on the coffee table and
said something about how the same power that raised Christ
from the grave will one day raise us, too, right along with Ms.
Edith in the embalming room next door. Brian took this as his
cue to pull us from the twilight zone into a familiar hymn he
strummed on his guitar, and our church of twenty—we called
ourselves the Mission—sang.

It wasn't exactly the catacombs. One of our members was
the daughter of the funeral director and she kept the spacious,

well-furnished suite homey and smelling of vanilla candles and clean laundry. Still, I felt like a modern-day Phoebe, renowned first-century deaconess of the house church at Rome, as I led the group through a piecemeal liturgy I'd extracted from *The Book of Common Prayer* with all the inchoate delight of an evangelical new to its gifts. Whenever Brian referred to me as the Mission's worship pastor, I flushed with pride.

We'd stumbled into these roles: I composed the liturgy and wrote whatever needed written. Brian cast the vision and won people over. Dan kept us legal and online. Carrie scouted out community service opportunities while resettling the Ward family in Dayton, Tennessee. Kaley, the funeral director's daughter, fed and sheltered us. And Matt and Jen, the final pair in what church-planting parlance termed our "core group," served as the treasurers of our paltry coffers.

At first, I had feared Brian and Dan might clash, as Brian's ministry mantra—"I just want to love on people"—remained unchanged from our youth group days, while Dan's—"Have we filed the necessary paperwork?"—evolved out of necessity. But with a little practice, the two grew to like one other. Dan's New Jersey grit is of the gentle sort, and I've never known anyone to remain uncharmed by Brian's easy, insouciant wit, which crackles like a bonfire and draws everyone around him into a circle of honesty and ease.

The voices joining our Easter chorus belonged mostly to twentysomethings who came after me in youth group—an odd mix of former back-row boys and Bible nerds, only now with spouses and even a baby or two in tow. Next to me sat a pair of Tea Party conservatives who made their impassioned opposition to immigration reform well-known on social media. On the other side of the room sat a couple that boasted an Obama '08 bumper sticker on their car. We bragged about our political and theological diversity and how it reflected our commitment to ultimate unity in Christ, but sometimes I wondered what would happen come the next election cycle . . . or a night when we had too much wine and someone brought up predestination or Obamacare.

Our greatest commonality was a desire to create a different sort of church in Dayton, namely by making it *authentic, intentional,* and *missional*—slippery buzzwords we said we hated, but which we still invoked from time to time because they reflected our truest hopes and dreams for the Mission. When we lingered at the deli downtown, dreaming big dreams over turkey sandwiches and fries, we talked about partnering with the local public schools for after-school tutoring programs, arranging our imagined sanctuary so that people sit around circular tables instead of in pews, sending a missions team to Uganda, curating exhibits for local artists, living simply so that others may simply live. We were idealistic and committed. We were hopeful and brave. We were being the change we seek in the world, and we were, to a person, broke.

The fistful of cash Dan and I contributed to the lawyer's fee when we filed the corporate nonprofit paperwork for the Mission felt as momentous as a down payment on a house. They say self-employment means living in famine or feast, and we were in the midst of famine fit to rival Pharaoh's nightmares. Brian and Carrie weren't much better off. Brian forfeited a comfortable megachurch salary to move to Dayton to start the Mission, working full-time in the Walmart automotive department changing people's oil and selling them tires.

The rest of our group was young and new to their jobs, new to their marriages, new to church planting. The majority of our income arrived in our PO box in little white envelopes from out-of-town donors who supported us like missionaries. We hoped that by summer, we would save enough to rent a place of our own downtown.

But until then, the funeral home apartment created an intimate atmosphere that invited people to settle in and stay. In the conversations following Brian's sermons, stories emerged of doubt, disillusionment, frustration, and hope. It was as if each week we shed one more layer of Southern pretense, slowly, carefully exposing our true selves. Christine, expressive and freckled with a sharp laugh and poetic mind, opened up about the abusive church she left and her ongoing struggle with shame and guilt. Kelly and Courtney, college students and roommates, talked about their adventures churchhopping in the Bible Belt. Dave and Liz asked for prayer for their finances, Jen for a healthy baby, Lisa that she'd pass the MCATs.

And on Easter, the light from the paschal candle made a halo on the ceiling that caught the marble blue eyes of little Aurora, our youngest member, who rested her head on her mother's chest. A joyful, expectant mood carried our prayers, as together we declared that "things which were cast down are being raised up, and things which had grown old are being made new, and that all things are being brought to their perfection by him through whom all things were made . . ."[34]

After prayers and worship, Brian preached from the book of John. He told us about the seven "I am" statements found in John's gospel and about how Jesus says he is the bread of life, the light of the world, the gate, the good shepherd, the vine, the way and the truth, the resurrection and the life. Brian said John's gospel uses the word *believe* more than any other and that John wrote his gospel "that you may believe that Jesus is the Messiah, the Son of God, and that by believing you may have life in his name." And for a moment, on this day of impossible things come true, I did. I believed more than I had in a long time.

June 2010

For our first baptism, we gathered on the banks of Chickamauga Lake, a muddy impoundment on the Tennessee River famous for its largemouth bass. A breeze rippled the water and stirred the cattails as Brian and Chad waded in, wearing T-shirts and swim shorts and squinting in the hot sun. Chad is one of Dayton's premiere electric guitar players and a staple in the local band scene. He had been following Jesus for a while, but with the Mission gaining momentum and his wedding just weeks away, he decided it was time to take the plunge.

From the water Brian made a joke the rest of us couldn't hear but that sent Chad into a fit of laughter, easing the awkward tension of the whole exercise (which, when you think about it, is indeed a little strange). "I baptize you in the name of the Father, the Son, and the Holy Spirit," Brian said before easing Chad under the water and back up again.

They hugged and slapped each other's backs, sending little showers of water through the air. We whistled and applauded from the shore while a family of ducks glided by unperturbed. Then we roasted hot dogs and grilled hamburgers and told our favorite stories from the old youth group days until the fireflies blinked in the grass. Everything smelled like summer—smoky and earthy and wet.

Later, there will be a wedding, a food drive, arguments, apologies, a baby shower, and a mission statement—the sort of things that turn an experimental community into a real church. We built the Mission on nights and weekends without much more than nickels and dimes; and at least at first, it seemed to work.

October 2010

On Halloween we hosted an open house at our new downtown storefront for the throngs of locals who descended upon the courthouse lawn for the annual Pumpkin Fest. They wandered in with squirmy little princesses and pirates on their hips, Joker masks pulled back over their heads, their eyes squinting and scanning our odd little space—fifteen feet wide and one hundred feet deep. "It looks like a bowling alley," they said, because it does.

We handed them mini chocolate bars and flyers and explained we were a church "committed to living out the Mission of God in community and for the community," and they were welcome to join us Sunday nights at seven. They smiled politely, but in a way that said, *just what this town needs—another church*, and I found myself resenting the fact that we spent four bucks a bag on that candy.

Despite Brian's connections at Walmart, we'd yet to make significant inroads in the broader community, and after several of our original members, including three couples, moved out of town, we stagnated. Still, work carried on at the new place, which the owner agreed to let us use for free if we helped him with some updates. We ripped out the banged-up pegboard to expose the brick. We purchased and installed toilets, painted walls, brought in used couches and armchairs to replace the folding metal chairs we endured with dramatic vexation for the first three weeks. We addressed the fluorescent light problem by utilizing Christmas lights, and borrowed floor lamps and the Japanese lanterns from Amanda's wedding. Dan even built a movable partition out of eighth-inch plywood to try and reign in the cavernous space, prompting him to joke that he was "dividing the church" and "building up walls." Our look was what you might call secondhand chic.

Chris and Tiffany were there, greeting everyone who walked through the door as if they were old friends . . . which they probably were. Chris teaches art at the local high school and Tiffany is a pharmacist, and between the two of them, they know everyone in town. When Matt and Jen took some time off for the baby, Chris and Tiffany volunteered to take over as treasurers of the Mission and since then we've become fast friends. Tiffany listens to NPR during each stretch of her lengthy daily commute, so she's the most informed person I know, comfortable discussing everything from college football to theology to US foreign policy with a thick East Tennessee accent and enviable vocabulary. Chris collects records and rides mountain bikes and cracks Dan up with his droll sense of humor and inventive use of profanity. They've got a bumper sticker on the back of their Volkswagen that says "not on the rug, man." We get along.

Chris and Tiffany chatted with a couple who attended one of Dayton's most prominent and conservative churches, and I wondered, darkly, if the couple was there to gather information. The Mission has been subjected to a surprising amount of gossip, even for Dayton, and I couldn't help but worry that it was my fault, that people who hated my blog had projected their disgust onto the whole church, which explained why it was rumored we taught evolution, didn't use our Bibles, drank like fish, and were almost entirely gay.

The fact that some people in town rooted for our demise made me all the more determined to prove them wrong, to keep working until our church was bigger and better than theirs and we *won*. But whenever I got all paranoid and tribal like that Brian called me out on it. We knew each other well enough now to see the blemishes and get under each other's skin. We were learning one another's quirks, one another's gifts, one another's go-to sins. (You're not a real church, I suppose, until you know one another's go-to sins.) We were holding one another accountable, but we were doing it as friends.

Brian reminded me this wasn't a competition. There was no Flush Valve Award to win this time around, no call to put people in their place. We wanted to define ourselves by what we were, he said, not by what we weren't.

I knew he was right. I knew it wasn't about winning but about serving. But as another couple wandered into the building and eyed our ragamuffin group with suspicion, I couldn't seem to shake the feeling that what we were wouldn't be enough.

February 2011

On our night to volunteer at the health clinic, Tiffany and I were tired. Building a church on nights and weekends was harder than it sounded, and the Mission was running out of money.

But the health clinic was a good idea. After donating school supplies and assembling Thanksgiving baskets, we wanted to engage in more consistent community service work through the Mission, so Carrie found Volunteers in Medicine, a clinic that provides nonemergency medical care to underprivileged patients free of charge. Doctors and nurses rotate in on Thursday nights, and volunteers work Tuesdays and Thursdays to greet patients, manage files, and sort through tax returns and other paperwork to see if prospective patients qualify for care. The place is run by a group of ladies from the Church of God, so much is said about God bringing the right people through the door and healing both physical and spiritual wounds, but it's all legit. People see actual doctors and get actual medicine. Tiffany and I tried to work the same nights so we could take turns managing the phones and working with patients.

I sat in an examining room with a toothless, rheumy-eyed man and his heavyset daughter who said her father had a heart condition that hadn't been treated by a doctor in years. They came the week before, I remembered, but without any information regarding his finances. At last they had returned with his latest tax return. I felt guilty about scrutinizing their plight with such lapidary care, calculator in hand, but these rules were in place when we arrived.

As I totaled up the household members and income, two people living on less than $20,000, I caught my breath. I'd just realized something.

"Good news," I said to the man sitting like a child on the examining table, his back hunched and his hands in his lap. "You qualify."

It wasn't until I got home that I told Dan: "I realized tonight that you and I would qualify too."

April 2011

Our last Sunday as the Mission fell on Easter. We met in the place downtown, now empty, cavernous and cold. There was no liturgy this time around, no paschal candle—just the ten of us who remained, standing in a circle, our hands on Brian and Carrie's shoulders, praying. It was a strange day to think about resurrection.

The Mission collapsed slowly, one week at a time, first as participation stagnated, then as it waned, then as it buckled under the financial strain. I saw the stress in Carrie's eyes and in Brian's shoulders, and I carried it into my own sleepless nights. There were no big fights, no dramatic exits. No one, that we know of, left disgruntled or hurt. A few of our members moved away, others burned out, and the rest of us stayed, even after the torpor set in, the inertia that comes with watching your time, money, and energy melt away. The building never seemed to get warm. When Brian said he needed to start looking for another job in ministry, one that would actually pay the bills, no one objected. He found one in Florida, at a United Methodist Church that needed a youth pastor, and he and Carrie and the girls would leave in just a few weeks.

Without much left to say, we decided to go around the room and share what we were grateful for. Chris and Tiffany were grateful that they made new friends, that their curiosity about Scripture had been piqued and engaged. Christine, wiping away tears, said the Mission became her sanctuary, a safe place to speak freely and recover from the last church experiences, and perhaps, to fortify her for the next. Kelly and Courtney were grateful for like-minded companionship, a chance to get off campus and really talk. The others mentioned the service projects, that time we pulled some money together to help a couple with rent, the baptism, the wedding, the communion services, the prayers, the inside jokes.

Carrie was grateful for how we loved on her girls, Brian for how we took a risk with him. Dan said he would do it all over again for the friendships we'd forged. I said the Mission was the first time I felt like an asset to the church instead of a liability, and I was glad that at least we tried, at least we took a risk.

Maybe you can't build a church on nights and weekends. But at least you can *be* one. At least you can love one another as well as you can in the midst of it.

Brian urged us to plug into other area churches after the Mission closed its doors, but the prospect of searching for another faith community left me feeling so exhausted, cynical, and lonely I couldn't imagine climbing out of bed on Sunday mornings ever again. It would be a few years before we would really even try.

As pink light filled the windows, we clasped one another's hands, concluding with our favorite prayer, adapted from Alcuin of York:

God, go with us. Help us to be an honor to the church.
Give us the grace to follow Christ's word,
to be clear in our task and careful in our speech.
Give us open hands and joyful hearts.
Let Christ be on our lips.
May our lives reflect a love of truth and compassion.
Let no one come to us and go away sad.
May we offer hope to the poor,
and solace to the disheartened.
Let us so walk before God's people,
that those who follow us might come into his kingdom.
Let us sow living seeds, words that are quick with life,
that faith may be the harvest in people's hearts.
In word and in example let your light shine
in the dark like the morning star.
Do not allow the wealth of the world or its enchantment
flatter us into silence as to your truth.
Do not permit the powerful, or judges,
or our dearest friends
to keep us from professing what is right.
Amen.

FIFTEEN

Epic Fail

All ministry begins at the ragged edges of our own pain.

—Ian Morgan Cron

THIRD AND WALNUT BAR IN LANSDALE, PENNSYLVANIA, used to be a church. When the church failed, the historic, two-story stone building was sold to an Elks Lodge, and then to a local businessman who hung lighted beer signs in the lancet windows and turned the church into a smoke-filled, hole-in-the-wall bar with karaoke on Wednesdays and live rockabilly music on Sundays. The bar changed hands a few times, closing and reopening. But in 2011, it caught the eye of a burned-out pastor named J. R. Briggs, who decided to use Third and Walnut as the venue for his first ever Epic Fail Pastors Conference.

"Considering the nature of the event," he said, "the location seemed perfect."

Like most crazy ideas, the Epic Fail Pastors Conference emerged spontaneously after Briggs confessed on his blog that the highly produced, expertly marketed pastors conferences featuring success stories from famous megachurch pastors left him feeling inadequate and depressed. Most ministers can't relate to overcrowded buildings and enormous marketing budgets, he said. Most ministers are just trying to make it through the day. In fact, a whopping 80 percent report being discouraged in their roles, and half say they would quit if they could.[35] But none of the conferences Briggs attended provided a safe place to talk about and process the ubiquitous reality of nearly every minister's life—failure.

"What if there was an EPIC FAIL Pastors Conference with the tag line 'where leaders put their worst foot forward?'" Briggs asked. "What if we led out of our weakness, not our strengths?"

To Briggs's surprise, within hours of posting the article, he received hundreds of comments, e-mails, and phone calls essentially saying, "I'd go."

And they did. Nearly one hundred pastors (and former pastors) from seventeen states descended upon Third and Walnut Bar to eat, drink, pray, and talk about what ministry is *actually* like. Writes Briggs:

> People shared their stories and struggles with refreshing courage. They opened up about their battles with depression and suicidal thoughts, their terror of failure and their broken hearts over a failed church nine years prior. They shared how dry, lost, and alone they felt. I looked at my watch. We were seventeen minutes in and people were standing up telling complete strangers stories of pain, loss, fear and deep wounds . . . There were no superstars, no impressive videos, no greenrooms and no lanyards . . . There was laughter and prayer and tears and refills. It was, as one retired pastor put it, "a kiss from God on our bruises."[36]

Ironically, the event was a success. Now Briggs hosts similar gatherings all over the country and has written a book entitled *Fail: Finding Hope and Grace in the Midst of Ministry Failure.*

It's strange that Christians so rarely talk about failure when we claim to follow a guy whose three-year ministry was cut short by his crucifixion. Stranger still is our fascination with so-called celebrity pastors whose personhood we flatten out and consume like the faces in the tabloid aisle. But as nearly every denomination in the United States faces declining membership and waning influence, Christians may need to get used to the idea of measuring significance by something other than money, fame, and power. No one ever said the fruit of the Spirit is *relevance* or *impact* or even *revival*. The fruit of the Spirit is love, joy, peace, patience, kindness, goodness, faithfulness, gentleness, and self-control—the sort of stuff that, let's face it, doesn't always sell.

I often wonder if the role of the clergy in this age is not to dispense information or guard the prestige of their authority, but rather to *go first*, to volunteer the truth about their sins, their dreams, their failures, and their fears in order to free others to do the same. Such an approach may repel the masses looking for easy answers from flawless leaders, but I think it might make more disciples of Jesus, and I think it might make healthier, happier pastors. There is a difference, after all, between preaching success and preaching resurrection. Our path is the muddier one.

It's been three years since the Mission's last Sunday and I'm still trying to figure out what went wrong. Was it our youth? Our lack of denominational backing? Our empty bank account? (All of the above?) I confess that when I play it all back in my mind, the whole undertaking reminds me of the old, jumpy film footage of man's failed attempts at flight, where someone's attached wings to a bicycle and peddled off a cliff. Any objective observer could have predicted our inevitable demise, and yet we barreled on, full of trust and hope and good intentions. I was as invested in a church as I'd ever been, and it failed. Epically.

And yet even our unsuccessful church plant managed to produce some fruit of the Spirit along the way. We baptized, broke bread, preached the Word, and confessed our sins. We created a sanctuary where people told the truth without fear. We fed the hungry and filled out paperwork with the sick. We worked through our differences with care and grace. And we learned, perhaps the hard way, that church isn't static. It's not a building, or a denomination, or a 501(c)(3) nonprofit organization. Church is a moment in time when the kingdom of God draws near, when a meal, a story, a song, an apology, and even a failure is made holy by the presence of Jesus among us and within us.

Church was alive and well long before we came up with the words *relevant* and *missional*, and church will go on long after the grass grows through our cathedral floors. The holy Trinity doesn't need our permission to carry on in their endlessly resourceful work of making all things new. That we are invited to catch even a glimpse of the splendor is grace. All of it, every breath and every second, is grace.

SIXTEEN

Feet

If you want to be holy, be kind.

—Frederick Buechner

FOR AS LONG AS ANYONE COULD REMEMBER, THE CER-
emonial foot washing had taken place at the grand Basilica of
St. John Lateran as part of the Holy Thursday Mass. The pope
would choose twelve priests, and in remembrance of Jesus'
act of service to his disciples, wash the priests' feet. But in
2013, just ten days after his election, Pope Francis stunned
the world and broke with tradition by traveling to a juvenile
detention center outside Rome where he washed and kissed
the feet of twelve prisoners, including two women and two
Muslims.

Traditionalists responded with angst to rival that of Peter,
particularly over the inclusion of women, but Francis had captured the attention of the world, reminding us that when Jesus
washed the feet of his friends, it was an act of humility and
love directed toward ordinary people, not merely a ceremony

observed by the religious elite. If washing feet was surprising then, why shouldn't it be surprising now?

When Jesus washed his disciples' feet, he was showing them what leadership in the upside-down kingdom of God looks like. He had told them before, when they squabbled over who would be the greatest in the kingdom, that while the kings and rulers of the world lorded their authority over their subordinates, he came not to be served but to serve, and if they wanted to follow his way, then they would have to do the same.

"You call me 'Teacher' and 'Lord,' and rightly so," Jesus told the disciples the night he washed their feet. "Now that I, your Lord and Teacher, have washed your feet, you also should wash one another's feet. I have set you an example that you should do as I have done for you" (John 13:13–15).

While Jesus calls all his followers to this style of humble leadership, most Christians hold in tension a belief in both the "priesthood of all believers" and the distinct calling of some Christians to specially ordained ministry roles. In many traditions, these roles—such as pastor, priest, deacon, and bishop—are known as holy orders, and ordination to them is considered a sacrament.

Unfortunately, the difference between the clergy and the laity is often perceived as more vast than it is, which leads to all sorts of trouble, from abusive and authoritarian churches, to the idolization of religious leaders by their followers, to unhealthy and unhappy pastors who struggle to manage the weight of the expectations placed upon them, to Christians who miss the full depth of their own callings because they believe ministry is something other people do.

Alexander Schmemann says, "If there are priests in the Church, if there is the priestly vocation in it, it is precisely in order to reveal to each vocation its priestly essence, to make the whole life of all men the liturgy of the Kingdom, to reveal the Church as the royal priesthood of the redeemed world."[37]

Ultimately, all Christians share the same calling. According to the apostle Peter, we are "royal priests," invited to "show others the goodness of God, for he called you out of the darkness into his wonderful light" (1 Peter 2:9 NLT).

Whenever we show others the goodness of God, whenever we follow our Teacher by imitating his posture of humble and ready service, our actions are sacred and ministerial. To be called into the priesthood, as all of us are, is to be called to a life of presence, of kindness.

My sister is like this—present and kind. No matter where she lives or travels, no matter what her vocation or responsibilities, Amanda inhabits a place with such a joyful and attentive openness it makes everyone around her a neighbor. When she lived in the city of Nashville, she worked with women caught in generational poverty, helping them find jobs, scouring the city for child care (or providing it herself), worrying with them about their GED scores, sharing in their jokes and celebrations, heartaches and breakdowns. When she lived in India for six months, she learned to sleep without air-conditioning and eat spicy Indian food, and by the time I visited her in Hyderabad, she had picked up some Telugu and knew the names of every single child in the school for HIV-affected kids where she served. The Indian family that hosted her grew so fond of her that they stayed in touch, even calling Amanda on her wedding day. They still talk regularly, and Amanda's been back to India three times, because for her, there's no such thing as a short-term missions trip.

Now she and her husband, Tim, live in Boone, North Carolina, where they both work for the humanitarian organization Samaritan's Purse. They also make sure to check in on

Miss Mary down the street, who has lived in the same mountain holler all her life and who gets by without electricity or living relatives, and they regularly invite people of all sorts into their home. Maybe I'm just a proud big sister, but when I think about the priesthood of all believers, I think about Amanda. And I think about Brian and Carrie Ward. I think about Pastor Doug and Pastor George. I think about Dan and Chris and Tiffany, and sometimes I even think of me.

"To be a priest," writes Barbara Brown Taylor, "is to know that things are not as they should be and yet to care for them the way they are."[38]

Such a purpose calls us far beyond our natural postures. It means surrendering all cynicism and pride to take up the basin and towel.

Just like my sister and the pope.

PART IV

Communion

SEVENTEEN

Bread

Give us each day our daily bread.

—Luke 11:3

AFTER THE RAIN, THE FARMER TILLED THE SOIL. ONE hand gripped the goad and the other steadied the plow as his oxen lumbered beneath the sun, furrowing the landscape with muddy ripples, brown as the wrinkles around his eyes. In autumn, hope tasted like sweat and smelled of ox and earth and manure. An experienced farmer kept his eyes on the heaving shoulders of the beasts ahead and used his weight to nudge the plowshare down a steady path. *No one who puts a hand to the plow and looks back*, the Teacher said, *is fit for service in the kingdom of God.*

After the tilling, the sower scattered seeds. Some seeds fell on rocky soil to be scorched by the sun, others fell on thorny soil to be choked out by the weeds, and still others were carried off by the wind to be eaten up by birds. But most sunk into the good soil where, in a tomb of darkness, they swelled and split open before breaking through the surface with a garish flash of green. *This is what the kingdom of God is like*, the Teacher said. *The seed sprouts and grows when the sower isn't watching.*

After the stalks grew tall and the heads heavy with grain, there was singing and dancing and harvest. Bodies bent like scythes inched through the fields, gathering the wheat into sheaves. The threshing floor echoed with the rhythmic pounding of flails as women with arms as strong as olive tree trunks loosened the grain from the chaff. At dusk, the children gathered to watch the winnowing forks pitch the last bit of chaff into the wind and send the rest of the bounty back to the earth like rain. *The harvest is plentiful*, the Teacher said, *but the workers are few.*

After the reaping, the hand mills hummed. This, too, was women's work—grinding grain into flour. Mother and daughter sat at the mill, spinning the handstone over the quern. It took all morning, but by noon a layer of white powder tickled their noses and speckled their hair. The mother teased the daughter about growing old in a day. *The kingdom of heaven is like yeast*, the Teacher said, *that a woman took and mixed into sixty pounds of flour until it worked all through the dough.*

Sixty pounds of flour! Imagine that.

After mixing the flour with water, the baker kneaded the dough. Her hands, calloused from the millstone grip and spotted from the sun, moved with quick precision as she folded and pressed and turned, folded and pressed and turned, folded and pressed and turned. Her surface was a simple wooden trough, her kitchen a modest courtyard, lit by the embers of a dying fire. Most of the time she added yeast and then waited for the dough to rise, but not on the days when her people remembered how liberation once caught them by surprise. On those days she sent it straight to the baking pan and watched until the top browned.

The scent made her stomach rumble. *I am the bread of life*, the Teacher said. *Whoever comes to me will never go hungry.*

What did he mean?

After the sun set, the servant brought up the bread. In one hand he balanced the loaves and the olive oil, in the other he carried a lamp to light his way up the stone stairs. His footsteps echoed too loudly, he thought, slowing down his pace. The mysterious company, once raucous with stories and songs, had quieted to sibilant whispers. Something about a betrayal. Something about a death. He kept his eyes on the floor as he approached the crowded table. But the Teacher thanked him before he took the bread and, like thousands of men in Jerusalem that night, lifted his eyes and said, *Blessed are thou, O Lord, our God, King of the Universe, who brings forth bread from the earth.*

The HaMotzi—the blessing of the bread and its journey from earth to table. The Greeks called this kind of thanksgiving *eucharisteo.*

After he blessed the bread, the Teacher broke it and said, *This is my body, given for you. Take it. Eat it. Don't ever forget.*

After he blessed the wine, the Teacher poured it and said, *This is my blood poured out for the forgiveness of sins. Take it. Drink it. Don't ever forget.*

After he left, the Teacher was arrested. After he was arrested, the Teacher was crucified. And after he was crucified, the Teacher was seen alive. They knew him by how he broke the bread.

After the Upper Room meal, the dog smelled the crumbs. His nose flared and his mouth watered as he scrambled up the stairs, paws scratching against the stone in frenzied patter. Soon he'd be chased out with a shout and a broom, but for a dog as skinny as he, even a few morsels would do. With animal abandon, he lapped up the spoils from under the table—some bread crumbs, a date, a scrap of fish, a few olives, and a taste of honey—before his ears perked to the far-off sound of another HaMotzi.

I am the living bread that came down from heaven, the Teacher said. *This bread is my flesh, which I will give for the life of the world.*

EIGHTEEN

The Meal

A family is a group of people who eat the same thing for dinner.

—Nora Ephron

THE FIRST THING THE WORLD KNEW ABOUT CHRISTIANS was that they ate together.

At the beginning of each week they gathered—rich and poor, slaves and free, Jews and Gentiles, women and men—to celebrate the day the whole world changed, to toast to resurrection. While each community worshipped a bit differently, it appears most practiced communion by enjoying a full meal together, with special prayers of thanksgiving, or *eucharisteo*, for the bread and wine.[39] They remembered Jesus with food, stories, laughter, tears, debate, discussion, and cleanup. They thanked God not only for the bread that came from the earth, but also for the Bread that came from heaven to nourish the whole world. According to church historians, the focus of these early communion services was not on Jesus' death, but rather on Jesus' friendship, his presence made palpable among his followers by the tastes, sounds, and smells he loved.

"With all the conceptual truths in the universe at his disposal," writes Barbara Brown Taylor, "[Jesus] did not give them something to think about together when he was gone. Instead, he gave them concrete things to do—specific ways of being together in their bodies—that would go on teaching them what they needed to know when he was no longer around to teach them himself . . . 'Do this,' he said—not *believe* this but *do* this—'in remembrance of me.'"[40]

So they did.

"They devoted themselves to the apostles' teaching," wrote Luke, "and to fellowship, to the breaking of bread and to prayer . . . All the believers were together and had everything in common. They sold property and possessions to give to anyone who had need . . . They broke bread in their homes and ate together with glad and sincere hearts, praising God" (Acts 2:42–47).

They were a ragtag bunch, for sure. The pagan writer Celsus dismissed Christianity as a silly religion, fit only for the uneducated, slaves, and women.[41] Indeed, sociological studies indicate most of the people drawn to the church in its first three centuries came from the lower echelons of society. Women, especially widows, found a home and occupation within the church, leading some to criticize it as too "effeminized" (proof that some things never change). There were strange rumors, too, rumors about purported love feasts that involved eating flesh and drinking blood—a mystery some said explained why Christians were so quick to take in orphans! But the religion of women and slaves continued to grow, even after its adherents were thrown to beasts in the arenas. In fact, persecution only seemed to grow it more.

Their unity wasn't always perfect, of course. In one of his letters, the apostle Paul offered a rather scathing correction to Christians in the church at Corinth who were apparently holding private, drunken feasts for the wealthy while the poor in their community went hungry. "My brothers and sisters," he pleaded, "when you gather to eat, you should all eat together" (1 Corinthians 11:33). The *Didache*, or *Teachings of the Twelve Apostles*, instructs Christians to settle their quarrels with one another before partaking of the meal. In some communities, the custom arose to send a piece of bread from the communion service at the bishop's church to other area churches to be added to the meal as a symbol of the bond of unity between all Christians.

Things changed when the emperor Constantine made Christianity the religion of the state and infused the Eucharist with imperial pomp and elements of pagan ceremony. Prayers grew more stylized and fixed. Solemn chants replaced the familiar hymns, vestured processions the mealtime banter. Christians no longer gathered around crowded tables but instead stood before altars of stone over which only priests could preside.[42] It was before the altar at Hagia Sophia that a cardinal from Rome read the sentence of excommunication that split in two the eastern and western churches. By the Middle Ages, many laypeople received the Eucharist only once a year.

Things changed again amidst the tumult of the Protestant Reformation. Some radical reformers dispensed with formal communion altogether and returned to the shared meals. Others kept elements of the tradition but shifted the focus of Sunday worship to preaching and teaching. Many rejected the Catholic doctrine of transubstantiation (that the bread and wine become the actual body and blood of Christ in communion), but could not agree on the exact manner of Christ's presence in the sacrament. Wars were fought and books were burned. You know how it goes.

Today the meal is known by many names—mass, holy communion, the Eucharist, the Lord's Supper—and is practiced in a myriad of ways. For some it marks the climax of every weekly gathering, for others it is observed just a few times a year. The bread might come as a hot loaf straight out of the oven, an oyster cracker nestled in the palm, or a thin wafer consecrated by a priest and placed directly on the tongue. The wine may be served from an ornamental chalice, a bottle passed around the table, or in rings of little plastic cups. (The wine may, in fact, be grape juice.)

The atmosphere might be celebratory or somber, the room filled with organ music or guitar strums, Gregorian chants or clinking silverware. In more liturgical traditions, the prayers are as familiar as the taste of the bread—"Let us lift up our hearts! We lift them up to the Lord!"—while in a Baptist church or a Bible church, the pastor may simply ask a member of the congregation to say grace.

The elements and the meal are identified in different ways: the body of Christ, broken; the blood of Christ, shed; the Bread of heaven, the cup of salvation, the mystery of faith, the supper of the Lamb. But in every tradition I know, someone, at some point, says, "Remember."

Remember how God became one of us? Remember how God ate with us and drank with us, laughed with us and cried with us? Remember how God suffered for us, and died for us, and gave his life for the life of the world? Remember? Remember?

"On those days when I have thought of giving up on church entirely," writes Nora Gallagher, "I have tried to figure out what I would do about Communion."[43]

Indeed it's easier to remember things together than alone.

As a child, I regarded communion with trepidation. Though

we marked it on the first Sunday of every month, seeing the silver plates stacked on the table at the front of the sanctuary always surprised and unnerved me. Our church had no confirmation process, so the timing of one's first communion was left to the discretion of one's parents. I hated having nothing to do while, in the silence following Pastor George's solemn recitation of Christ's words from the Last Supper, I could hear everyone in the room chewing, swallowing, and gulping down their oyster crackers and grape juice in one loud cacophony of ingestion. When I finally got the nod from my mother to go ahead and partake, I was so horrified by the sound of my own loud chewing, which rang like a garbage compactor in my ears, that I took to slipping the oyster cracker under my tongue and letting it dissolve through the rest of the service so as not to disturb the entire congregation with my clamorous manducation. To this day I have to remind myself to actually eat the thing.

It was the Anglican tradition that reconnected me to the beauty of the Eucharist, as it does for so many. I once visited an Episcopal church in Louisville, Kentucky, where the entire sanctuary was built around the table. It sat right in the center of the sunlit room, on a raised, circular chancel, surrounded by pews forming a semicircle on one side, and by the choir, lectern, and pulpit on the other—the perfect visual expression of the eucharistic thrust of Anglican liturgy.

"Whoever comes to me shall not hunger," we sang before circling the table together. "And whoever believes in me shall never thirst."

"The gifts of God for the people of God," said the priest, as she raised the bread and wine above her pregnant belly. "Take them in remembrance that Christ died for you, and feed on Christ in your hearts by faith, with thanksgiving."

While our various ceremonial remembrances of the meal

may be meaningful in their own right, it's a shame they aren't accompanied more often by actual feasts, complete with bread baskets and wine bottles, elbows and spills, cleanup and candle- light, and big fat serving bowls of mashed potatoes, corn on the cob, and fresh green beans. For many, such feasts are a staple of their informal church life—those planned or impromptu gatherings around Chinese takeout or a backyard grill when the people of God just hang out together—but the dichotomy between the sacred and the secular is a Western construction, and one I suspect those first disciples of Jesus would find a bit curious given what we know about those first Sunday meals.

At a church called St. Lydia's in New York City, pastor Emily Scott is trying to change that. On Sunday and Monday nights, crowds of around thirty gather together in a storefront in Brooklyn to cook and share a meal together. Affiliated with the Evangelical Lutheran Church in America, this "dinner church" brings together ancient Christian practices with mod- ern, urban living.

The service begins with the lighting of candles and the sing- ing of hymns. Some in the group already know one another; others are strangers, at least at the start. In the kitchen, the main course—often a vegetarian soup or stew—simmers on the stove. After the hymns, a pastor leads the group in a sung eucharistic prayer from the earliest days of the church. Each person stands around the giant table with hands lifted. "As grain was scattered across the hills, then gathered and made one in this bread, so may your church, scattered to the ends of the earth, be gathered and made one in your commonwealth . . ."

The pastor breaks a hot loaf of bread and sends the two pieces around the table. As the bread is shared around the room, the participants say to one another, "This is my body. Remember."

Then the meal is served. Holy food for holy people. The conversation picks up as introductions, stories, jokes, and drinks are shared. Sometimes the discussion flows freely. Other times it is awkward. Always, it is interesting.

After the meal, a deacon or pastor reads Scripture and preaches a brief sermon, before inviting congregants to share their own stories around the theme. Prayers and petitions are made. And then, at the end of the meal, the group blesses the cup. "Remember, Lord, to deliver your church from all evil and teach it to love you perfectly. You have made it holy; now build it up and gather it from the four winds into the realm you have prepared for it . . ."

The rest of the evening is filled with washing, rinsing, drying, and storing the dishes as guests work together to clean up. Worship concludes with a hymn, offering, and light dessert. No one leaves a stranger.

"We do church this way because people are hungry," Emily explains. "People in New York have hungry bellies that may be filled with home-cooked food. They have hungry souls that may be filled with holy text, holy conversation. And these hungers are sated when we come together and eat.

"We do church this way," she says, "because people are looking for Jesus. People are looking for Jesus and thinking that just maybe they see him, but then again maybe not. But when we sit down together and break bread, we glimpse him for a moment in one another's eyes and say to each other, 'I see Christ at this table; I see him when we sit down together and eat.'"[44]

The gospel of Luke recounts a story in which two of Jesus' disciples encountered a stranger on the seven-mile stretch of road from Jerusalem to Emmaus. When he asked why they appeared so downtrodden and anxious, the disciples told the stranger about the events that had transpired in Jerusalem that week, about how their Teacher had been betrayed, abandoned, crucified, buried, and—according to some dubious rumors purported by the women—brought back to life again. As the stranger walked with them, he explained how these things represented a fulfillment of Scripture. But it was not until they arrived at Emmaus and shared a meal together that the disciples realized the stranger was more than a fellow journeyman or prophet. When he broke the bread and gave thanks, "their eyes were opened and they recognized him" (Luke 24:31). It was Jesus!

Something about communion triggers our memory and helps us see things as they really are. Something about communion opens our eyes to Jesus at the table.

As I was editing this chapter, a beloved aunt died suddenly from a staph infection that spread to her spine without warning. A healthy and active seventy-two-year-old, she had just returned from a Mediterranean cruise with my uncle when what began as backache left her totally paralyzed and on life support within hours. I caught a plane to Iowa to grieve with family and friends, all of us numbed by shock. As we gathered at my aunt and uncle's home, the doorbell rang every few hours as another member of First Baptist Church showed up with a casserole of cold cuts, fresh fruit and bread, homemade ice cream and pies of every variety—a veritable cavalcade of Iowa home cooking. (In Iowa, by the way, Jell-O is considered a salad.) Over these meals, we found the strength to cry, to share memories, to express our disbelief, and to laugh deeply and loudly as my cousin Michael recounted the time he and his best friend snuck into the church's bell tower and replaced the tape of recorded chimes with AC/DC's "Hell's Bells."

"That's the lady who served us communion at church this morning," my dad said, as a woman stood in the doorway, wrapping my uncle in a hug with one arm and balancing a stack of Tupperware in the other.

"And here she is, serving it again," I replied.

Like Gallagher, on the days when I contemplate leaving Christianity, I have wondered what I would do without communion. Certainly nonbelievers can care for one another and make one another food. But it is Christians who recognize this act as sacrament, as holy. It is Christians who believe bread can satisfy not only physical hunger, but spiritual and emotional hunger, too, and whose collective memory brings Jesus back to life in every breaking of the bread and pouring of the wine, in all the tastes, smells, and sounds God himself loves.

NINETEEN

Methodist Dance Party

People who love to eat are always the best people.

—Julia Child

I DIDN'T KNOW I WAS HUNGRY.

In the midst of grappling with the failure of the Mission, I experienced some modest professional success with the publication of my second book, which sent me travelling around the country speaking at colleges, churches, and conferences about the church, Bible, gender equality, and media. This new itinerate lifestyle provided the perfect cover for not looking for a new church—how could we when we weren't even in town most weekends?—and distracted me from the nagging emptiness that accompanies a dream deferred. It also reintroduced me to the people of the church universal, who, at a time when I felt like a religious orphan, welcomed me, supported me, listened to me, and, of course, fed me.

The Methodists of Jackson, Tennessee, served barbecue and coleslaw at their women's retreat. The Baptists of Houston,

Texas, brought in food trucks so we could picnic over Tex-Mex on the church lawn. I threw back shots of tequila with a van full of Presbyterian pastors as our taxi sped along the coastline of Cozumel, Mexico. I tried the iced cowboy coffee at Common Grounds in Waco, while a gaggle of Baylor University students waited for the thumbs-up.

In Grand Rapids, a reader named Caroline handed me a stack of salted dark chocolate chip cookies tied up in a baby-blue bow, which made such an impression I now know the recipe by heart. In Seattle, Pastor Tim and his husband Patrick served up fresh salmon with avocado mango salsa, asparagus, quinoa, and local red wine. In Cochabamba, Bolivia, a guinea pig farmer welcomed our team of World Vision bloggers into her one-room home with meal of boiled potatoes, which we passed around like communion bread. In Holland, Michigan, the Dutch Reformed grilled up hot dogs and hamburgers and sent me home with a pair of wooden shoes.

I shared homemade bread and jam with the Quakers of Portland, shrimp and grits with the Wesleyan Foundation of Williamsburg, macaroni and cheese with the Mennonites of Harrisonburg, Virginia, and melt-in-your-mouth roasted chicken and mashed potatoes with the Dominican nuns of Siena Heights. The Free Methodists of Greenville, Illinois, introduced me to Adam Brothers homemade chicken noodle soup, for which I still get insatiable cravings whenever I'm sick. The Disciples of Christ took me to my first In-N-Out Burger, where I pretended to have the religious experience they expected. I even ate blueberry pancakes at the White House, where, at the annual Easter Prayer Breakfast, civil rights leader Otis Moss gave the best sermon on resurrection I've ever heard in my life. I dined with rocket scientists and musicians, Bible scholars and activists, rabbis and priests, monks and nuns, the homeless and the wealthy, professional chefs and home cooks. I may have gained a few pounds.

"Food is a language of care," writes Shauna Niequist, "the thing we do when traditional language fails."[45]

The end of the Mission felt like something of a death, and whether these good people knew it or not, they were caring for me in my grief. In exchange, I delivered some passable sermons and lectures and tried to answer people's questions during panel discussions and Q&As. Not a single group was rude or inattentive, but sometimes I felt in over my head. Like the time I had to tell a room full of Presbyterian seminarians I did not in fact have an opinion about *supersessionism* because I had no idea what *supersessionism* is. (They seemed to find this response acceptable, as Presbyterians generally oppose *supersessionism*, which I take to mean they're against Texas leaving the union.) Or the time I realized, a little too late, that Churches of Christ and United Church of Christ are not, in fact, the same denomination . . . not by a long shot.

But never did my insecurities rage more violently than when I was asked to speak at youth events. Though much has changed since the Chubby Bunny days, youth events remain the *pièce de résistance* of extrovert culture. There are strobe lights and fog machines, skits and talent contests, rope courses and altar calls and games. Hundreds of teenagers bounce to the throbbing pulse of theologically questionable worship songs while the back-row boys look on. Ankles will be broken. Romances will be kindled. T-shirts will be shot from cannons. At some point, a guy wearing skinny jeans and a dozen rubber wristbands will jump on the stage and tell everyone in the audience to find someone they don't know and give them a giant Jesus-hug. When I am introduced, he will say, "Rachel Held Evans is here to BLOW YOUR MIND!"

I will not blow their minds.

"Honestly, teenagers aren't my typical audience," I told the youth pastors who called to invite me to speak.

"Yes, but you've got a very popular blog," they said.

"You realize my last post was a three thousand–word discussion on biblical regulations regarding menstruation, right? I don't have a ton of suitable material for middle school boys."

"Well maybe don't talk about your period."

"You sure you want me to do this?"

"Absolutely."

"Can you assure me there will be no fog machines?"

"I'm afraid we've already ordered them."

One such conversation led me to Eagle Eyrie, a four hundred–acre wooded camp in Lynchburg, Virginia, where youth from the Virginia Conference of the United Methodist Church have been holding their annual fall retreat for decades. I was asked to speak at all four of the main sessions, to around five hundred junior high and high school students, around the theme of "Living the Questions."

As the first group of students streamed out of their church vans like ants from a disturbed bed, I marveled at their young faces and worried fresh over my severe lack of cool. It occurred to me that the youngest of these students had been toddlers on September 11, 2001. Toddlers! What made me think we were even asking the same questions?

I spent the week leading up to the conference reworking all my usual material, calling Brian Ward for advice, and scouring the Internet to see what the kids are into these days.

"Be sure to be funny," my friends said. "Teenagers like funny."

"Work in some pop culture references," they said. "Talk about music and movies they know."

"Don't even think about using PowerPoint!"

"It's best not to stick with a script."

"You've got exactly fifteen minutes before you lose them. Whatever you do, don't go over."

"Just don't try too hard," Brian warned. "They see right through that. They know when you're faking it."

So I just had to be funny, hip, and concise—without really trying. Got it.

Despite all the preparation, I panicked when I took the stage after the band finished the first night, streams of water vapor still clinging to the set, five hundred young faces looking back at me. Before I approached the microphone, I closed my eyes and prayed: *God, just help me do right by these kids, just help me do right by these kids, just help me do right by these kids.* After a few seconds of silence, I cleared my throat, chuckled nervously, and confessed I was a little nervous. No faking it, right?

The first presentation went okay. The students laughed at my jokes and only a few fell asleep. I didn't talk about my period. And as the weekend went on, I started to get the hang of things. I learned the students' names and listened to their feedback. I developed a friendly banter with some of the older kids, especially the boys who were surprised to get permission from their female chapel speaker to interrupt the next session with an update on the Alabama football game.

The climax of the weekend happened on Saturday night with a communion service for all the students, volunteers, chaperones, and ministers. A Methodist pastor presided over the table, but asked me and a few of the student leaders to help distribute the bread and wine.

As I stood at the front of the rustic camp meeting room, holding a loaf of bread in one hand and tearing off a piece at a time with the other, hundreds of people approached, one at a time, with their hands held out, ready to receive.

"This is Christ's body, broken for you," I said.

I said it over and over again, to each person who came to the table—to the back-row boys who avoided my gaze, to the girls whose mascara rivered down their cheeks, to the kids who giggled in line with their friends, to the ones who came all alone.

This is Christ's body, broken for you.

I said to the ones wearing designer jeans, to ones with beat-up shoes, to the ones I could tell were athletes, to the ones who were clearly the class clowns, to the ones who probably got picked on in school.

This is Christ's body, broken for you.

I said it to the skinny girl who reached for a hug, the youth leader with tired red eyes, the chaperones who mouthed words of thanks.

This is Christ's body, broken for you.

I said it to the boy who approached with his walker, the jock who grinned and whispered "Roll Tide," the mom who told me she sent a letter of complaint to the UMC when she heard I was going to be the speaker.

This is Christ's body, broken for you.

There were wrinkled hands and pierced noses and flashes of brilliant white teeth against chocolate skin. There were babies on hips, Band-Aids on fingers, hands in pockets, nervous shuffles, and teary eyes.

This is Christ's body, broken for you.

In the faces that passed by I saw joy, relief, anxiety, boredom, shyness, familiarity, distraction, and hope. I saw broken families, fights with friends, doubts about God, and insecurities about the van ride home.

This is Christ's body, broken for you.
This is Christ's body, broken for you.
This is Christ's body, broken for you.

I said it more than three hundred times—until at last I believed it, at last I understood: it wasn't my job to do right by these kids; this wasn't about me at all. I could only proclaim the great mystery of faith—that Christ has died, Christ has risen, and Christ will come again, and that somehow, some way, this is *enough*. This body and this blood is *enough*.

At Eagle Eyrie I learned why it's so important for pastors to serve communion. It's important because it steals the show. It's important because it shoves you and your ego and your expectations out of the way so Jesus can do his thing. It reminds you that grace is as abundant as tears and faith as simple as food.

"When [Jesus] wanted fully to explain what his forthcoming death was all about," writes New Testament scholar N. T. Wright, "he didn't give a theory. He didn't even give them a set of scriptural texts. He gave them a meal."[46]

I guess sometimes you just have to taste and see.

After the service, we celebrated with a light show and dance party, because that's how the Methodists roll. I busted out my worst dance moves to the cheers of the students, wholly unconcerned about my lack of cool. Somewhere between the choruses of "We Are Young" and "Call Me Maybe," I realized how much I needed these teenagers from Virginia, the ones I had once thought needed me. Communion has a way of flattening things out like that, a way of entangling our roots and joining our hands.

On the days when I am hungry—for community, for peace, for belief—I remember what it was like to feed people Jesus, and for people to feed Jesus to me. And those pieces of memory multiply, like the bread that fed the five thousand, spilling out of their baskets and filling every hollow space. Communion doesn't answer every question, nor does it keep my stomach from rumbling from time to time, but I have found that it is enough. It is always and ever enough.

TWENTY

Open Hands

It's dangerous, opening your hands.

—Nora Gallagher

I RESIST IT EVERY TIME.

All the way down the aisle and up the steps to the altar I fidget, folding and unfolding my arms, clasping and unclasping my hands, forcing my mouth into a pleasant, inconspicuous smile as my eyes greet the faces of the congregants who have gone before me.

There is organ and choir and stifled coughs and babies' cries.

There is incense and hair spray and old church and cheap perfume.

My knees hit the pillow beneath the altar rail and light from the stained glass dapples my skin. It's as vulnerable a posture as a body can assume: kneeling, hands cupped together and turned out—expectant, empty, exposed—waiting to receive. I resist it every time, this childlike surrender, this public reification of *need*.

Prayer, at least, offers some protection with its clasped hands, bowed heads, closed eyes. But here at the table I am open, unsheltered. The lines on my palms are dry creek beds in a basin awaiting water. I am a little girl crouched beneath the spigot.

The Body of Christ, the Bread of Heaven.

Jesus descends into my open hands.

The Blood of Christ, the Cup of Salvation.

Jesus slips in, through my parted lips.

"If we did nothing else," writes Nora Gallagher, "if nothing was placed in our hands, we would have done two-thirds of what needed to be done. Which is to admit that we simply do not have all the answers; we simply do not have all the power. It is, as the saying goes, 'out of our hands.'"

"Faith," she says, "is a catch-and-release sport. And standing at the altar receiving the bread and wine is the release part."[47]

But I'm no good at the releasing and receiving, at least not without practice. Ours is a culture of achievement, of sufficiency, of bootstrap pulling and ladder climbing. We celebrate the winners, the leaders, the do-it-yourselfers. Like any good American, I like to wait until I think I've *earned*. I like to wait until I think I've *deserved*. With giving, I can maintain some sense of power, some illusion of control. But receiving means the gig is up. Receiving means I'm not the boss of what comes into life—be it trial or trouble or unmerited good.

A writer friend of mine recently sent me a bouquet of orchids that sat on our dining room table for weeks in a perpetual explosion of magenta. She sent them because she knew I was in one of those seasons when I wanted little to do with God and nothing to do with the church. Christians had been cruel to one another and cruel to me, and it had all happened in a public forum. I was in no mood to accept any acts of mercy, particularly from the very sort of Christians against whom I was revolting. Embarrassed by her generosity, I sent a quick thank-you in response and resolved to return the favor sometime. If I owed her, maybe I wouldn't have to let her in.

I was in possession of my friend's gift long before I received it, on a gray day when its stubborn, irresponsible beauty could no longer be ignored. Until then, I didn't want to admit how badly I needed her kindness, how helpless I was at sorting all this out on my own. I didn't want to see myself in those fragile, thirsty orchids, fighting against the gloom to trestle toward the light.

But this friend knows better than most the nature of *eucharisteo*—thanksgiving—how it enters through our soft spots and seeps in through our cracks. She knew God would unclench my fists and unfurl my fingers and that grace would eventually get through.

And so it did, when I finally opened my hands, when I received grace the way I receive communion, with nothing to offer back but thanks.

"Grace cannot prevail," writes Robert Farrar Capon, "until our lifelong certainty that someone is keeping score has run out of steam and collapsed."[48]

This is why I need the Eucharist.

I need the Eucharist because I need to begin each week with open hands.

I need the Eucharist because I need to practice letting go and letting in.

I need the Eucharist because I need to quit keeping score.

"No one has been 'worthy' to receive communion," writes Alexander Schmemann, "no one has been prepared for it. At this point all merits, all righteousness, all devotions disappear and dissolve. Life comes again to us as Gift, a free and divine gift . . . Everything is free, nothing is due and yet all is given. And, therefore, the greatest humility and obedience is to accept the gift, to say yes—in joy and gratitude."[49]

It's a scary thing to open your hands. It's a scary thing to receive, to say yes. I resist it every time. But somehow, whether it sneaks in through a piece of bread, a sip of wine, or a hatching bud, grace always, eventually gets through. And finally, at long last, I exhale my thanksgiving.

TWENTY-ONE

Open Table

You are loved, someone said. Take that and eat it.

—Mary Karr

WHEN SARA MILES WAS FORTY-SIX, SHE WANDERED INTO an unfamiliar church, ate a piece of bread, and took a sip of wine. Until that moment she'd had no interest in religion. Traveled, liberal, and lesbian, she was raised in a secular home and remained deeply skeptical of what she'd seen of the church, particularly its more fundamentalist iterations. She'd never been baptized, never read much of the Bible, never prayed the Lord's Prayer. But at St. Gregory's of Nyssa Episcopal Church in San Francisco, someone invited Sara to the table.

"And then something outrageous and terrifying happened," she says. "Jesus happened to me."[50]

Sara felt dizzy, overwhelmed, charged with life, filled. Suddenly, she believed.

"I couldn't reconcile the experience with anything I knew or had been told," Sara writes in her memoir, *Take This Bread*.

"But neither could I go away: For some inexplicable reason, I wanted that bread again. I wanted it all the next day after my first communion, and the next week, and the next. It was a sensation as urgent as physical hunger, pulling me back to the table."

So with the bewildered support of her partner and daughter, Sara went back to St. Gregory's—the next Sunday, and the Sunday after that, and the Sunday after that. Not only did she convert to Christianity, she devoted herself entirely to "a religion rooted in the most ordinary yet subversive practice: a dinner table where everyone is welcome, where the despised and outcasts are honored."[51]

Sara partnered with St. Gregory's to create a massive food pantry, where the poor, elderly, sick, homeless, and marginalized from the community are served each week from the very table where Sara took her first communion—no strings attached, no questions asked. With the saints painted on the walls looking on, hundreds gather around the communion table to fill their bags with fruit, vegetables, rice, beans, cereal, bread, canned goods, peanut butter, and whatever happens to be in the five-to-six-ton bounty of food that particular Friday. Many become volunteers themselves, joining church staff for a meal together at noon.

The food pantry recalls a conversation Jesus once had with a group of religious leaders at the home of a prominent Pharisee. "When you give a banquet," Jesus said to his host, "invite the crippled, the lame, the blind, and you will be blessed." He told them a parable about a man who prepared a banquet and invited many guests. When those on the guest list declined to attend, the man instructed his servant to go into the streets and alleyways in town and bring back the poor, the hungry, the handicapped, and the lonely. The servant obeyed, but told his master there was still room at the table. "Then go out to the roads and country lanes and compel them to come," the master said, "so that my house will be full" (Luke 14:12–23). This is what God's kingdom is like: a bunch of outcasts and oddballs gathered at a table, not because they are rich or worthy or good, but because they are hungry, because they said *yes*. And there's always room for more.

"Holy communion knocked me upside down and forced me to deal with the impossible reality of God," Sara writes. "Then, as conversion continued, relentlessly challenging my assumptions about religion and politics and meaning, God forced me to deal with all kinds of other people . . . I wound up not in what church people like to call 'a community of believers'—which tends to be code for 'a like-minded club'—but in something huger and wilder than I had ever expected: the suffering, fractious, and unboundaried body of Christ."[52]

Not surprisingly, Sara advocates for what's called an open table, the practice of inviting all who are physically or spiritually hungry to participate in communion, regardless of religious background or status. Most churches maintain some requirements regarding who may partake of the bread and wine—typically, that they be baptized—a tradition adopted early on in the church's history, but which would have excluded Sara from that first powerful Eucharist experience and which would leave out many of the poor and sick she serves.

Though I have never been part of a church that hosts an open table, I'm with Sara on this one. I don't know exactly *how* Jesus is present in the bread and wine, but I believe Jesus *is* present, so it seems counterintuitive to tell people they have to wait and meet him someplace else before they meet him at the table. If people are hungry, let them come and eat. If they are thirsty, let them come and drink. It's not my table anyway. It's not my

denomination's table or my church's table. *It's Christ's table.*
Christ sends out the invitations, and if he has to run through the
streets gathering up the riffraff to fill up his house, then that's
exactly what he'll do. Who am I to try and block the door?

Long enshrined traditions around communion aside, there
are always folks who fancy themselves bouncers to the heavenly
banquet, charged with keeping the wrong people away from
the table and out of the church. Evangelicalism in particular
has seen a resurgence in border patrol Christianity in recent
years, as alliances and coalitions formed around shared theological distinctives elevate secondary issues to primary ones
and declare anyone who fails to conform to their strict set of
beliefs and behaviors unfit for Christian fellowship. Committed
to purifying the church of every errant thought, difference of
opinion, or variation in practice, these self-appointed gate-
keepers tie up heavy loads of legalistic rules and place them on
weary people's shoulders. They strain out the gnats in everyone
else's theology while swallowing their own camel-sized incon-
sistencies. They slam the door of the kingdom in people's faces
and tell them to come back when they are sober, back on their
feet, Republican, Reformed, doubtless, submissive, straight.

But the gospel doesn't need a coalition devoted to keeping
the wrong people out. It needs a family of sinners, saved by
grace, committed to tearing down the walls, throwing open the
doors, and shouting, "Welcome! There's bread and wine. Come
eat with us and talk." This isn't a kingdom for the worthy; it's a
kingdom for the hungry.

The compulsion to keep a pure, homogeneous table is an
old one, reflective of ingrained social customs and taboos that
surround communal eating. The English word *companion* is
derived from the Latin *com* ("with") and *panis* ("bread").[53] A
companion, therefore, is someone with whom you share your

bread. When we want to know about a person's friends and associates, we look at the people with whom she eats, and when we want to measure someone's social status against our own, we look at the sort of dinner parties to which he gets invited. Most of us prefer to eat with people who are like us, with shared background, values, socioeconomic status, ethnicity, beliefs, and tastes, or perhaps with people we want to be like, people who make us feel important and esteemed. Just as a bad ingredient may contaminate a meal, we often fear bad company may contaminate our reputation or our comfort. This is why Jesus' critics repeatedly drew attention to the fact that he dined with tax collectors and sinners. By eating with the poor, the despised, the sick, the sinners, the outcasts, and the unclean, Jesus was saying, "These are my companions. These are my friends." It was just the sort of behavior that got him killed.

The apostle Peter continued this pattern, but took it even further by daring to dine with Gentiles. As a Jew, keeping kosher was tantamount to Peter's very faith and identity, but when following Jesus led him to the homes and tables of Gentiles, Peter had a vision in which God told him not to let rules—even biblical ones—keep him from loving his neighbor. So when Peter was invited to the home of Cornelius, a Roman centurion, he declared: "You are well aware that it is against our law for a Jew to associate with or visit a Gentile. But God has shown me that I should not call anyone impure or unclean" (Acts 10:28). Sometimes the most radical act of Christian obedience is to share a meal with someone new.

The Right Reverend Michael Curry, bishop of the Episcopal Diocese of North Carolina, tells the story of a young woman who became an Episcopalian in the 1940s. One Sunday, she invited the man she had been dating to join her at morning services. Both of them were African American, but the church they attended that day was all white, and right in the heart of segregated America. The young man waited in the pews while the congregation went forward to receive communion, anxious because he noticed that everyone in the congregation was drinking from the same chalice. He had never seen black people and white people drink from the same water fountain, much less the same cup. His eye stayed on his girlfriend as, after receiving the bread, she waited for the cup. Finally, the priest lowered it to her lips and said, as he had to the others, "The blood of our Lord Jesus Christ, which was shed for thee, preserve thy body and soul unto everlasting life." The man decided that any church where black and white drank from the same cup had discovered something powerful, something he wanted to be a part of.

The couple was Bishop Curry's parents.

Communion, Curry says, "is a sacrament of unity that overcomes even the deepest estrangements between human beings."[54]

"Participation in the Lord's Supper," writes Richard Beck, "is an inherently moral act. In the first century church, and in our own time, people who would never have associated with each other in the larger society sit as equals around the Table of the Lord . . . The Eucharist, therefore, is not simply a symbolic expansion of the moral circle. The Lord's Supper becomes a profoundly subversive political event in the lives of the participants. The sacrament brings real people—divided in the larger world—into a sweaty, intimate, flesh-and-blood embrace where 'there shall be no difference between them and the rest.'"[55]

I would be lying if I said I relished this "sweaty, intimate, flesh-and-blood embrace" without reservation. Sure, I'm happy to pass the bread to someone like Sara Miles or the neighbor who mows our lawn when we're out of town. But Sarah Palin?

Glenn Beck? Those gatekeeper types I was just talking about? Not so much. On a given Sunday morning I might spot six or seven people who have wronged or hurt me, people whose politics, theology, or personalities drive me crazy. The church is positively crawling with people who don't deserve to be here . . . starting with me.

But the table can transform even our enemies into companions. The table reminds us that, as brothers and sisters adopted into God's family and invited to God's banquet, we're stuck with each other; we're family. We might as well make peace. The table teaches us that faith isn't about being right or good or in agreement. Faith is about feeding and being fed.

Perhaps this is why so many of Scripture's most powerful eschatological visions include images of feasting. "On this mountain the LORD Almighty will prepare a feast of rich food for all peoples," declared the prophet Isaiah, "a banquet of aged wine—the best of meats and the finest of wines" (Isaiah 25:6). "People will come from east and west and north and south," Jesus said, "and will take their places at the feast in the kingdom of God" (Luke 13:29). John's vision at Patmos climaxes with the declaration, "Blessed are those who are invited to the wedding supper of the Lamb!" This heavenly banquet includes "a great multitude that no one could count, from every nation, tribe, people and language . . . Never again will they hunger; never again will they thirst" (Revelation 19:9; 7:9, 16). Christians believe the fulfillment of God's dreams for the world—the *eschaton*—is marked by a feast in which no one is hungry and all who gather are companions.

In my struggle to find church, I've often felt that if I could just find the right denomination or the right congregation, if I could just become the right person or believe the right things, then my search would be over at last. But right's got nothing to do with it. Waiting around for right will leave you waiting around forever.

The church is God saying: "I'm throwing a banquet, and all these mismatched, messed-up people are invited. Here, have some wine."

TWENTY-TWO

Wine

Oh, taste and see that the LORD is good!

—Psalm 34:8 ESV

EARLY IN HIS MINISTRY, BEFORE CROWDS, RUMORS, AND threats followed him everywhere, Jesus attended a wedding at Cana. It was just the sort of event the man was known to love, packed with eating and drinking, music and laughter, the scent of roasted lamb mingling with the perfume of flower garlands, the sweet taste of pomegranate, raisins, dates, and honey, the roar of animated conversations between family and friends punctuated by the music of bangles clinking around the women's wrists. In first-century Palestine, even modest weddings were marked by three to four days of feasting. So when the wine ran out, the hosts—probably close relatives of Jesus without much money to spare—faced serious social embarrassment.

Wine in this era was not a luxury. The scarcity of water, and its frequent contamination, made wine a necessity for cooking, nourishment, and hospitality. Along with grain and oil, the presence of wine indicated God's blessing on a community, while its absence signaled a curse. Wine was a staple, the stuff of life.

Concerned for their hosts, Mary informed Jesus of the situation, apparently expecting her son to do something in response. According to John's account, Jesus resisted at first, but in an odd exchange that I suspect would make more sense if we had the benefit of observing facial expressions and tone, Jesus changed his mind. (Even the Messiah, it seems, obeys his mama.) He instructed the servants to fill six empty stone pots with water. Used for Jewish purification rituals, each pot held twenty to thirty gallons, and the servants filled them to the brim. When the party-planner drew from the pots to take a sip, he couldn't believe it. The water had turned to wine! And 150 gallons of it, far more than they would ever need. This, John reports, "was the first of the signs through which [Jesus] revealed his glory" (2:11).

It was a strange way to start a ministry—turning water into wine. And what sort of sign is it anyway, ensuring that a simple wedding feast carry on?

It may be tempting to dismiss the miracle and Cana as a mere magic trick, an example of Jesus flexing his messianic muscles before getting to the real work of restoring sight to the blind and helping the paralyzed off their mats. But this is only because we have such a hard time believing that God cares about our routine realities, that God's glory resides in the stuff of everyday life, just waiting to be seen.

"God works through life, through people, and through physical, tangible and material reality to communicate his healing presence in our lives," explains Robert E. Webber when describing the principle of sacrament. "God does not meet us outside of life in an esoteric manner. Rather, he meets us through life incidents, and particularly through the sacraments of the church. Sacrament, then, is a way of encountering the mystery."[56]

This is the purpose of the sacraments, of the church—to help us *see*, to point to the bread and wine, the orchids and the food pantries, the post-funeral potlucks and the post-communion dance parties, and say: pay attention, this stuff matters; these things are holy.

"Sacredness requires specificity," says Milton Brasher-Cunningham, a minister and chef. "The grand esoteric themes of theology have their place, but love takes root in those specific moments when we voluntarily and intentionally enter one another's pain."[57]

Or enter one another's joy, one another's family, one another's messes, one another's suppers.

Indeed, the word *sacrament* is derived from a Latin phrase which means "to make holy." When hit with the glint of love's light, even ordinary things become holy. And when received with open hands in the spirit of *eucharisteo*, the signs and wonders of Jesus never cease. The 150-plus gallons of wine at Cana point to a generous God, a God who never runs out of holy things. This is the God who, much to the chagrin of Jonah, saved the rebellious city of Nineveh, the God who turned five loaves of bread and a couple of fish into a lunch to feed five thousand with baskets of leftovers to spare. This God is like a vineyard manager who pays a full day's wage for just one hour of work, or like a shepherd who leaves his flock in search of a single lamb, or like a father who welcomes his prodigal son home with a robe, a ring, and a feast.

We have the choice, every day, to join in the revelry, to imbibe the sweet wine of undeserved grace, or to pout like Jonah, argue fairness like the vineyard employees, resent our own family like the prodigal's older brother. At its best, the church administers the sacraments by feeding, healing, forgiving, comforting, and welcoming home the people God loves. At its worst, the church withholds the sacraments in an attempt to lock God in a theology, a list of rules, a doctrinal statement, a building.

But our God is in the business of transforming ordinary things into holy things, scraps of food into feasts and empty purification vessels into fountains of fine wine. This God knows his way around the world, so there's no need to fear, no need to withhold, no need to stake a claim. There's always enough—just taste and see. There's always and ever enough.

PART V

Confirmation

TWENTY-THREE

Breath

Jesus said, "Peace be with you! As the Father has sent me, I am sending you." And with that he breathed on them and said, "Receive the Holy Spirit."

—John 20:21–22

THE SPIRIT IS LIKE BREATH, AS CLOSE AS THE LUNGS, THE chest, the lips, the fogged canvas where little fingers draw hearts, the tide that rises and falls twenty-three thousand times a day in a rhythm so intimate we forget to notice until it enervates or until a supine yogi says *pay attention* and its fragile power awes again. Inhale. Exhale. Expand. Release. In the beginning, God breathed. And the dust breathed back enough oxygen, water, and carbon dioxide to make an atmosphere, to make a man. Job knew life as "the breath of God in my nostrils," given and taken away. With breath, the Creator kindled the stars, parted a sea, woke a valley of dry bones, inspired a sacred text. So, too, the Spirit, inhaled and exhaled in a million quotidian ways, animates, revives, nourishes, sustains, speaks. It is as near as the nose and as everywhere as the air, so *pay attention.*

The Spirit is like fire, deceptively polite in its dance atop the wax and wick of our church candles, but wild and mercurial as a storm when unleashed. Fire holds no single shape, no single form. It can roar through a forest or fulminate in a cannon. It can glow in hot coals or flit about in embers. But it cannot be held. The living know it indirectly—through heat, through light, through tendrils of smoke snaking through the sky, through the scent of burning wood, through the itch of ash in the eye. Fire consumes. It creates in its destroying and destroys in its creating. The furnace that smelts the ore drives off slag, and the flame that refines the metal purifies the gold. The fire that torches a centuries-old tree can crack open her cones and spill out their seeds. When God led his people through the wilderness, the Spirit blazed in a fire that rested over the tabernacle each night. And when God made the church, the Spirit blazed in little fires that rested over his people's heads. "Quench not the Spirit," the apostle wrote. It is as necessary and as dangerous as fire, so stay alert; *pay attention.*

The Spirit is like a seal, an emblem bearing the family crest, a promise of belonging, protection, favor. Like a signet ring to soft wax, the Spirit impresses the supple heart with the power and prestige of God, and no one—not kings, not presidents, not the wealthy, nor the magisterium—can take that identity away. The bond of God is made of viscous stuff. He has put his seal on us, wrote the apostle, and given us his Spirit in our hearts as a guarantee (2 Corinthians 1:22). In the rite of confirmation, which acknowledges the presence of the Spirit in a believer's life, a thumb to the forehead reminds God's children of their mark: the seal of the gift of the Holy Spirit. It's as invisible as your breath but as certain as your skin, *so pay attention*; don't forget who you are.

The Spirit is like wind, earth's oldest sojourner, which in one place readies a sail, in another whittles a rock, in another commands the trees to bow, in another gently lifts a bridal veil. Wind knows no perimeter. The wildest of all wild things, it travels to every corner of a cornerless world and amplifies the atmosphere. It smells like honeysuckle, curry, smoke, sea. It feels like a kiss, a breath, a burn, a sting. It can whisper or whistle or roar, bend and break and inflate. It can be harnessed, but never stopped or contained; its effects observed while its essence remains unseen. To chase the wind is folly, they say, to try and tame it the very definition of futility. "The wind blows wherever it pleases," Jesus said. "You hear its sound, but you cannot tell where it comes from or where it is going. So it is with everyone born of the Spirit" (John 3:8). We are born into a windy world, where the Spirit is steady as a breeze and as strong as a hurricane. There is no city, no village, no wilderness where you cannot find it, so *pay attention*.

The Spirit is like a bird, fragile alloy of heaven and earth, where wind and feather and flight meet breath and blood and bones. The rabbis imagined her as a pigeon, the Celts a wild goose. Like a dove, she glided over the primordial waters, hovered above Mary's womb, and descended onto Jesus' dripping wet head. She protected Israel like an eagle, and like a hen, brooded over her chicks. "Hide me in the shadow of your wings," the poet king wrote. "Because you are my help, I sing in the shadow of your wings" (Psalm 17:8, 63:7). The Spirit is as common as a cooing pigeon and transcendent as a high-flying eagle. So look up and sing back, catch the light of God in a diaphanous scrim of wing. *Pay attention.*

The Spirit is like a womb, from which the living are born again. We emerge—lashes still wet from the water, eyes unadjusted to the light—into a reanimated and freshly charged world. There are so many new things to see, so many gifts to give and receive, so many miracles to baffle and amaze, if only we *pay attention*, if only we let the Spirit surprise and God catch our breath.

TWENTY-FOUR

Wayside Shrines

How far I have to go to find you in
whom I have already arrived!

—Thomas Merton

FOUR MONTHS AFTER THE MISSION'S LAST SUNDAY, I sped down Route 278 in Northwest Alabama, the windows of the Acclaim rolled all the way down and Gillian Welch singing the Elvis Presley blues from the speakers. A hot August sun summoned fingers of steam from the asphalt that grabbed vainly at my tires as they tumbled past another tractor supply store, another barbecue joint, another Baptist church. The air conditioner didn't work—at least not without shrill objections from the compressor belt—but the morning air was redolent of earth and pine and cool enough as long as I kept moving. With each mile marker that whizzed by, the sun rose higher in the sky and the destination ahead grew sharper in my imagination.

"All guests who present themselves are to be welcomed as Christ," St. Benedict wrote in his *Rule*, which has guided fifteen centuries of monastic life for monks and nuns across the world. "Proper honor must be shown to all, especially to those who share our faith and to pilgrims."

Perhaps it was this promise of an open door that inspired my pilgrimage to St. Bernard Abbey in Cullman, Alabama—a quiet Benedictine monastery hidden in eight hundred acres of loblolly pines. Or maybe, after what seemed in hindsight like a recklessly untethered church-planting enterprise, I longed for something anchored, something old.

Built in 1891 by German immigrants whose community dated back to the 700s, St. Bernard houses a community of around twenty monks, a prep school, a hospitality center, and the famous Ave Maria Grotto—a sprawling, folk art–style miniature village created by resident Brother Joseph in the 1920s and '30s and a popular tourist attraction for people who like sprawling, folk art–style miniature villages, or who are on their way to Florida and need a stretch. I'd called ahead to secure a room within the monastery, which I found simple but well-appointed and mercifully cool, thanks to a window unit that greeted me with a cheery, guttural yawn. The guestmaster left the key hanging from a thumbtack on a corkboard in one of the compound's vast and silent hallways, where the air itself seemed fragile enough to break. I blushed as each of my steps echoed like gunfire in the deserted cloister, certain the sound waves alone were enough to topple the porcelain Virgin watching from the glass table in the corner. For a moment I wondered if a three-day visit was too ambitious, if even a lifelong introvert could stay this *still*.

I found my way to the church about an hour before evening mass and settled into a back pew. Afternoon light poured in through the wide clerestory windows, setting the sandstone walls, columns, and parabolic arches aglow. Ahead, a ten-foot

Byzantine-style crucifix hung suspended over the stone altar, depicting Christ crucified on one side and Christ victorious on the other. The ceiling above, made of stained Alabama pine, reminded me of Bible Chapel, or of the hull of a ship, upturned. Below was a blue slate floor, dark and cold as the sea.

Carved into the columns that flanked the nave, as if supporting the sanctuary with their shoulders, were the figures of ten saints. Among them were John the Baptist, looking frazzled as always with his disheveled hair and protruding ribs, King David holding a lyre and crown, St. Boniface wearing a scowl and brandishing the ax he used to cut down the oaks of pagan worship, and St. Bernard, the monastery's patron, bearing both a crosier and a sword, his role as an apologist for the failed second crusade unforgotten even among his fans. (I confess I had rather hoped to see a portrayal of the Lactation of St. Bernard, the oft-depicted scene from a legend in which the saint kneeled before a nursing Madonna and was hit with a squirt of milk from her breasts, curing him of an eye infection. The image always makes me smile.)

It was a Monday, so as the five o'clock hour approached, only a few gathered for mass. A smattering of students, teachers, and parishioners walked in one by one, dipping their fingers in stoups of holy water, crossing themselves, and genuflecting before the crucifix before finding places in the pews, their bodies spaced out like the pieces on a chessboard at the end of a game. Finally, a line of robed monks filed into the choir, took their places, and began to chant. Their voices rose and receded like the shadows playing on the walls, and it was as if the sanctuary suddenly woke up, its stones inhaling and exhaling the timbre of ancient, holy songs.

"Glory to God in the highest. And on earth peace to men of good will. We praise you. We bless you. We adore you . . ."

"Holy, holy, holy Lord God of hosts. Heaven and earth are full of your glory . . ."

"Lamb of God, you take away the sins of the world, have mercy on us . . ."

I fumbled my way through the Kyrie, Gloria, and Sanctus, watching the people around me for cues for when to kneel, cross myself, and mumble along. Everything proceeded with a sort of hushed routine, a shared familiarity that made me feel like a tourist to these people's faith. The Catholic Church discourages non-Catholics from receiving the Eucharist, so I remained in my seat as the twenty or so congregants approached the altar to receive the elements. The "Not Catholic?" part of my brochure suggested I use this moment to "pray for the reunification of the church," which, though I'm sure it was unintended, sounded a lot like, "You sit here and think about that schism you caused."

It wasn't until the next afternoon—after the monks chanted through Vespers at the conclusion of mass, after dinner was taken in silence in the refectory, after we sang the sweet prayers of Compline together in the empty and darkened church, after the Grand Silence of the night hours, after struggling to make it to Morning Prayer at six a.m., after a silent breakfast, after two glorious hours spent reading Julian of Norwich in the sunshine by the lake, after accidentally locking myself out of my room—that I actually had a conversation with someone.

"I've just been dying to talk to you!" said Susan, the blonde, middle-aged woman with a Virginia accent who sat across from me at the guest table at lunch. She spooled her spaghetti around her fork with attentive vim, her nails painted magenta, a tangle of gold and silver bracelets catching the light. "Well, I've been dying to talk to anyone, really. I didn't realize they kept silence during breakfast and dinner."

"Silent breakfast is fine by me," I said. "I'm not exactly a morning person."

Susan released a generous peal of laughter, startling an elderly monk at the other table. "I don't like silent anything. And yet here I am! But isn't this place wonderful? I mean, you can positively *feel* the presence of the saints in every room. When my husband said he had business in Irondale and wanted me to come along, I found this place on the Internet and took it as a sign."

Irondale was a solid hour away, but Susan struck me as the type to take everything as a sign.

"And what brings you here?" she asked, her face pinned with delighted expectancy.

"I'm a writer from the Chattanooga area, and I've been studying the subject of silence for a project I'm working on. So I thought: what better place to learn about silence than a Benedictine monastery?"

Just as I had rehearsed. No mention of books (or they ask for titles), no mention of the blog (or they assume I'm a mom), no mention of religion (or they get weird). You don't become a Silver Medallion member with Delta without learning a few things about small talk.

"Isn't that fascinating?" Susan cried. "Maybe you can get this place some publicity!"

At that moment we were joined by Brother Brendan, the quiet and bespectacled monk who served as the guestmaster.

"Rachel here is a writer," Susan said.

"That's wonderful," said Brother Brendan. "It's a joy to have you with us, Rachel."

"I'm not Catholic," I said, regretting it instantly. For some reason I wanted to get that out of the way, to divulge it up front, lest I be found out through some clumsy, accidental sacrilege and thought a imposter. But the announcement came out as abrupt, defensive.

Brother Brendan seemed unfazed and went about carefully sprinkling salt on his spaghetti, but Susan looked as though I'd just informed her I'd been orphaned.

"Oh. Are you a . . . person of faith?" She fingered her necklace protectively—a silver Jesus on a gold cross.

"Oh yes. Definitely."

"And where do you attend . . . services?"

"Well, I grew up evangelical, but I've been rethinking things lately. Our last church sort of dissolved, which was a painful experience. Now I'm not sure what I am. I guess you might say I'm searching."

Before the words left my mouth, I knew I'd just violated rule number one of conversational self-preservation: never tell a religious person you're searching.

Susan seized the moment. She told me about her favorite Catholic writers, jotted down the names of four books she thought might help me in my quest, and shared her own story of growing up Catholic, leaving for a while, and coming back again, drawn, she said, by the feminine presence of Mary, which helped her heal from a difficult childhood. My inner Protestant carped now and then, but I found myself moved by her sincerity and impressed by her knowledge of Christian history and theology.

"Do you ever doubt?" I asked both Susan and Brother Brendan.

It is a question I often ask of the devout, and I can always guess the answer within seconds of posing it. For those who have doubted, a flash of warm recognition spreads across their faces, as if they've just discovered we share an alma mater, a hobby, or an old friend. Those who haven't look back at me perplexed, like I've begun speaking Swahili.

Neither Susan nor Brother Brendan had ever doubted.

"In fact," said Brother Brendan, "my faith was strengthened after the tornado."

Months before, in April, an F-4 had rolled through Cullman, ripping the roof off the county courthouse, leveling several homes and businesses, and killing three people. Upturned oaks and maples lined Route 278, their maze of ancient roots exposed, and signs advertising shingles and roof repair stippled the farmland. Overgrown driveways led to heaps of siding and Masonite that, were it not for the foundations and inexplicably erect mailboxes, you would never guess had once been homes.

"It came so close to campus we could hear it roaring," Brother Brendan said, as Susan leaned in closer, eyes wide. "All around was destruction, and yet we didn't lose a single tree."

"It was the blessed Mother's protection," Susan whispered.

They looked at me, expecting some kind of a response, but I didn't know how to tell them this was exactly the sort of thing that made me doubt. Christians like to claim divine protection when a long line at Starbucks miraculously saves them from the fourteen-car pileup on the interstate, or when a wildfire just misses their home to take out a dozen others, but I'm always left wondering about the victims, those whose supposed lack of faith or luck or significance puts them in the path of the tornado instead. What kind of God pulls storm clouds away from a church and pushes them toward a mobile home park? And what kind of Mother would only shield a few if her arms were wide enough to cover all?

I studied my plate, feeling both guilty for asking these questions and resentful of those who don't. No matter where I went to church, I realized, doubt would follow, nipping at my heels. No matter what hymns I sang, what prayers I prayed, what doctrinal statements I signed, I would always feel like an outsider, a stranger.

"It's a miracle nothing was damaged," I finally said, wondering for the first time what exactly I'd hoped to find in this place.

....

August in Alabama isn't something you trifle with. It's the time of year newspapers across the South run dozens of stories about kids passing out at football practice and band camp, punctuated with sidebars extolling the virtues of proper hydration. So after a brief stroll through the grounds of St. Bernard following lunch, I escaped to the abbey chapel, which, in the stifling afternoon heat, waited cool and quiet as a cave.

With the place to myself, I ambled through the sanctuary, studying every window, alcove, icon, and plaque, listening to the church tell her story. A journey through a church, though a modest pilgrimage, can be an instructive one if you pay attention, if you follow the signs.

The floor plan took the shape of the Latin cross, with the massive stone altar at the crossing. In the north transept rested the veiled tabernacle, which housed the Eucharist—"God made present for us in food," the guidebook said. In the south transept sat two confessionals, over which shone the Holy Spirit window, depicting the familiar white dove amidst a swirl of red, blue, gold, and green. The east end, by the choir, boasted a forty-four–rank pipe organ of approximately 2,400 pipes, the west the resurrection window—a modern piece made of rows of little stained-glass squares. But the soaring parabolic arches, clerestory lights, and everything about the place drew the eyes upward toward the centerpiece: the flat Byzantine-style cross, suspended over the altar as if in amber trimmed with gold. On the side facing the congregation was Christ crucified, the scene painted in dreary black, copper, and brown tones. On the side facing the choir was Christ victorious, levitating in a bright blue sky spotted with gold stars, a white robe over his shoulder and a medallion of the Sacred Heart blazing as a seal on his chest.

Along the north and south aisles, twelve alcoves corresponding with the twelve stations of the cross invited visitors into prayer and meditation with icons, candles, prayer benches, and artwork. In one I found a moving *pietà*, a reproduction of a thirteenth-century wood carving in which Mary holds a broken Jesus in her arms, every mother's anguish etched into her face. In another, I found a statue of the Infant of Prague, which unnerved me at first, having never seen baby Jesus so royally decked out before. In another I found a pricket stand lined with red votive candles. I slipped a dollar's worth of very loud quarters through the slot for donations, struck a match, and lit three—one for healing for a sister-in-law diagnosed with breast cancer; one for thanksgiving for my friend Ahava, who weeks before had left a prayer for me in the Western Wall; and one to acknowledge a relationship in need of repair. The flames shimmied and waved, moved by the rhythm of unseen currents in the air. I lit one more candle for myself, calling to mind the words of Milton, "What in me is dark, illumine." Then I knelt on the prayer bench, put my head in my hands, and in the quiet of that sacred space, talked to God.

It's funny how, after all those years attending youth events with light shows and bands, after all the contemporary Christian music and contemporary Christian books, after all the updated technology and dynamic speakers and missional enterprises and relevant marketing strategies designed to make Christianity cool, all I wanted from the church when I was ready to give it up was a quiet sanctuary and some candles. All I wanted was a safe place to *be*. Like so many, I was in search of sanctuary.

During mass, I watched a young Latino family go forward for communion—the woman veiled with a mantilla, a cooing toddler in her arms, her husband's hand on her back—and was surprised by the hot tears that ran down my cheeks. They approached the altar with such confidence, such joy. How I longed to be as at home in my faith. How I longed to be so sure of my footing.

Benedictines recite the psalms every day, at morning, noon, and evening prayers, working through the entire Psalter every few weeks. Immersing themselves in the rhythm and imagery of these ancient songs brings the power and pathos of Scripture to life, for the psalms have a way of reminding the reader—or, in this case, the chanters—that whatever joy, agony, fear, delight, or frustration one is experiencing at the moment has, in fact, been experienced before. In this sense, a psalm can be both intimate and communal, deeply personal and profoundly universal.

At Vespers that night, in the company of twenty men who had taken vows of poverty, chastity, community, work, and prayer, and with whom I seemed to have so little in common, I intoned the words of Psalm 39:

> *Show me, Lord, my life's end*
> *and the number of my days;*
> *let me know how fleeting my life is.*
> *You have made my days a mere handbreadth;*
> *the span of my years is as nothing before you.*
> *Everyone is but a breath,*
> *even those who seem secure . . .*

Hear my prayer, LORD,
listen to my cry for help;
do not be deaf to my weeping.
I dwell with you as a foreigner,
a stranger, as all my ancestors were.
Look away from me, that I may enjoy life again
before I depart and am no more.

And even in the Grand Silence that followed, I felt a little less alone.

....

I nearly skipped a tour of the famed Ave Maria Grotto on my last day at St. Bernard. It cost seven bucks to see and I'd already gone all Martin Luther on the gift shop, scandalized over the sale of holy water, which, when you think about it, isn't much different than evangelicals selling *Duck Dynasty*-themed Bibles in their bookstores, but still . . .

Thankfully, a blue sky and a generous breeze beckoned me, and a smattering of other tourists plus a tabby cat, down the shady trail that meanders through the strange and charming world of Brother Joseph Zoettle.

Brother Joseph came to St. Bernard from Bavaria in 1892, when he was just fourteen. Informed by the abbot that he could never fulfill his dream of becoming a priest because his hunchback proved too much of a distraction, Joseph was put to work, first in the quarry on the grounds of the abbey, then as a traveling housekeeper to parishes across the Southeast (including, I learned, Dayton, Tennessee), and finally as the keeper of the abbey's powerhouse—a job that left him stoking fires, shoveling coal, monitoring gauges, and troubleshooting all manner of malfunctions, often for seventeen hours a day. Joseph hated the work, and wasn't shy about sharing his troubles in his journals and with his fellow monks. But in 1918 he discovered the writings of Thérèse of Lisieux, whose famous "little way" inspired him to go about even his menial tasks with love.

Beginning with a single small grotto near the quarry, Joseph used his precious free time to fashion miniature buildings and shrines out of concrete, glass, trinkets, and an array of discarded building materials. When his Little Jerusalem began attracting visitors from outside the abbey, the abbot asked Joseph to make miniature grottos to sell for charity. Joseph made more than five thousand such pieces before he was finally released, at age fifty-four, to devote the rest of his life to tending his tiny world. By the time he died in 1961, Brother Joseph had cobbled together Jerusalem, Bethlehem, St. Peter's Basilica, the Monte Casino Abbey, the Leaning Tower of Pisa, the Hanging Gardens of Babylon, and more than 120 other grottos, markers, towers, and shrines spread out over four acres, each constructed from an amalgam of stones and shells, cement and chicken wire, marbles and ash trays, jewelry and tiles, even toilet bowl floats—gifts to Brother Joseph from pilgrims from around the world.

The monk still watches over the place, his slumped shoulders and impish face preserved in a bronze statue near the entrance of the now famous site, collectively known as the Ave Maria Grotto, after its seminal work. In the black-and-white photos in the museum, Brother Joseph wears overalls, a poor-boy hat, and a furrowed brow—exactly how I imagine an elderly Owen Meany.

At first, the unapologetic ebullience of the site overwhelms. One gets the sense that Brother Joseph responded to every creative challenge he encountered by adding just a bit . . . *more*.

The result is an explosion of cement, color, and religious kitsch that at once amuses and confounds. Wandering down the concrete steps, I turned my camera first to a miniature Tower of Babel dotted with mosaic tiles, then to a crucifix made of blue ink bottles, then to a gaudy shrine built around a tiny souvenir-style Statue of Liberty, then to a seashell-encrusted birdbath out of which grew a bouquet of dessert bowls attached to "stems" of iron rods. The tabby cat followed close behind, scratching her back on the Sanctuary of Our Lady of Lourdes before peeing all over the Parthenon. Next I found Hansel and Gretel's Temple of the Fairies, a crowd favorite, featuring a tiny pumice organ fit for a grasshopper, an altar and baptismal font made of cold cream jars, and a winged cement dragon with red marble eyes hiding in the basement.

There was a certain playfulness about the haphazard arrangement of things, with St. Peter's Basilica (its dome made from a birdcage) sharing a neighborhood with the Alamo. And there was a tenderness in the details: the potted cacti around the Spanish missions, the designated chipmunk crossing drawn across the path, the veterans' memorial lined with dozens of tiny crosses "in memory of the St. Bernard boys killed in World War II." The on-site literature acknowledged that the scale of Brother Joseph's miniatures are noticeably distorted—towers, buttresses, and doorways too large or too small—but the monk's inspiration came almost entirely from postcards and books. He walked the streets of Jerusalem, Rome, and Paris only in his mind.

At the center of the garden stood Brother Joseph's magnum opus—an artificial cave made of concrete, stone, and shells, twenty-seven feet deep and twenty-seven feet tall, where Our Lady of Prompt Succor was assaulted by a lightning storm of white marble stalactites. (Brother Joseph hit the proverbial jackpot when a train derailed on the L&N about twenty miles from Cullman, and he scored a freight car full of damaged marble.) Rococo meets folk art proved a bit much for me; I wasn't sure where to point my camera. My self-guided tour concluded with the Tower of Thanks, a lopsided cement spire inlaid with shells and topped with four glass balls—sea green in the sunlight—once used as fishing net floats in Ireland.

It was a lot to take in, but along the trail I developed a special affinity for the site's many wayside shrines. Spaced out at the intervals in the path, they represented some of the artist's most charming and inventive work and imitated similar roadside markers that are common across Europe. Often erected on highways that lead to popular pilgrimage sites, wayside shrines resemble birdhouses or tabernacles and, according to my guidebook, "provide a place for travelers to stop and offer praise, turning heart and mind to God." They signal to the pilgrim that he's on the right path and invite him to worship right where he is.

While the wayside shrines of Europe typically house images of Jesus, Mary, and the saints, Brother Joseph, of course, added his own flourishes, haloing his subjects with bottle caps, marbles, costume jewelry, and hermit crab shells. I stopped at each shrine and smiled, their presence something of an affirmation that pilgrimage isn't always a bad idea, that even here, in a garden of kitschy folk art in Cullman, Alabama, I was on the right path.

From one, a ceramic bust of Jesus that Brother Joseph probably picked up from a gas station somewhere looked back at me, and with a goofy grin more befitting the Dude than the Son of God, seemed to say, "Keep going, Rachel. Don't be in such a hurry. Remember I am with you always, even to the end of the world."

I took a picture and said a prayer of thanks—for St. Bernard Abbey, for the Mission, for Grace Bible Church, for Bible Chapel, for youth events and college chapels and airport prayer rooms and Christian conferences, for the Methodists of Jackson, for the Baptists of Waco, for the Catholic monks of Alabama, even for Presbyterians, for the Catedral Metropolitana San Sebastián in Cochabamba, Bolivia, for the Chapel of the Transfiguration in Grand Teton National Park, and for all the wayside shrines of this world where I've found sanctuary, if even just for a time.

Madeleine L'Engle said, "the great thing about getting older is that you don't lose all the other ages you've been."[58] I think the same is true for churches. Each one stays with us, even after we've left, adding layer after layer to the palimpsest of our faith.

Thanks to evangelicalism, I don't need Google to tell me that the book of Ezra follows 2 Chronicles or where to find the words *love is patient, love is kind.* Thanks to the emerging church, I know I'm not the only one who doubts or the only one who dreams of beating swords into plowshares and spears into pruning hooks. Were it not for the Anglicans, I'd have never found *The Book of Common Prayer* or fallen in love with the Eucharist. Were it not for the Mission, I'd have never known the depth of my own resourcefulness or the importance of taking risks.

The journey comes with baggage, yes. And heartbreak. But there are also many gifts. In a sense, we're all cobblers. We're all a bit like Brother Joseph, piecing together our faith, one shard of broken glass at a time.

Just a week after my trip to St. Bernard, I visited a Quaker community where one of its members, a barefoot young man with a ponytail, put it this way: "I spent a lot of years journeying through a bunch of religious traditions, looking for a place where I fit. But now I feel perfectly at home here with the Friends, or in a Catholic mass, or swaying and clapping at the AME church down the road. When the Spirit lives within you, any place can become a sanctuary. You just have to listen. You just have to *pay attention*."[59]

....

The difference between a labyrinth and a maze is that a labyrinth has no dead ends.

The famed eleven-circuit labyrinth inlaid in the floor of Chartres Cathedral in France has just one path, which takes the pilgrim in and out of four quadrants in a spiraling motion through dozens of left and right turns, before reaching its rosette center. Such a pattern invites meditation, the mystics say, and reminds the pilgrim the journey of faith is rarely a straightforward one.

It has become cliché to talk about faith as a journey, and yet the metaphor holds. Scripture doesn't speak of people who *found* God. Scripture speaks of people who *walked* with God. This is a keep-moving, one-foot-in-front-of-the-other, who-knows-what's-next deal, and you never exactly arrive. I don't know if the path's all drawn out ahead of time, or if it corkscrews with each step like in Alice's Wonderland, or if, as some like to say, we make the road by walking, but I believe the journey is more labyrinth than maze. No step taken in faith is wasted, not by a God who makes all things new.

"To become aware of the possibility of the search is to be onto something," said Walker Percy. "Not to be onto something is to be in despair."[60]

I thought about this as I emerged from Brother Joseph's Ave Maria Grotto, threw my duffle bag in the back of the

Acclaim, and headed back up Route 278 away from St. Bernard Abbey toward home. I didn't know what was next in my search for church, but I knew I was onto something. It was either just around the next bend or a million miles away. Or maybe somewhere in between. But when the wind's at your back, you keep moving. You press on.

TWENTY-FIVE

Trembling Giant

How monotonously alike all the great tyrants and conquerors have been. How gloriously different are the saints!

—C. S. Lewis

ONE OF THE OLDEST LIVING THINGS IN THE WORLD IS A clonal colony of quaking aspen in Fish Lake, Utah, called Pando. Estimated to be around eighty thousand years old (though no one knows the exact age for certain), Pando is a favorite October entry for wall calendars, as no photographer can resist those stark white trunks and shimmering golden leaves set against the shocking sapphire of a cloudless autumn sky. But Pando can be deceptive, for as artist Rachel Sussman puts it, "what looks like a forest is, in a sense, a single tree."[61] In truth, Pando comprises a massive underground root system and each of its forty-seven thousand trees are but stems springing from that system, making Pando one enormous, genetically identical organism. And a male one at that. He's nicknamed the Trembling Giant.

At last count, there are nearly as many denominations in Christianity as there are trees growing from Pando. Each one looks different—beautiful and broken in its own way—but we all share the same DNA.

We tend to lament this seemingly endless parceling of Christianity (which, let's face it, can indeed get out of hand), but I'm not convinced the pursuit of greater unity means rejecting denominationalism altogether. A worldwide movement of more than two billion people reaching every continent and spanning thousands of cultures for over two thousand years can't expect homogeneity. And the notion that a single tradition owns the lockbox on truth is laughable, especially when the truth we're talking is *God*.

We might instead think of the various Christians traditions as different facets of a diamond refracting the same light, or as workers tending to a shared garden but with unique tasks, or as a single body made of many interconnected parts (1 Corinthians 12). Our differences can be cause for celebration when we believe the same Spirit that sings through a pipe organ can sing through an electric guitar, a Gregorian chant, or a gospel choir—though perhaps not at the same time!—and that we each hear the Spirit best at a different pitch.

In his book *Manifold Witness*, John R. Franke writes, "The many parts of the church are called to participate together in a unity characterized by *interdependent particularity*. Each is a part, and only a part, of the embodied witness to truth of the gospel made known in Jesus Christ. Each plays its part by bearing faithful witness to Jesus Christ in all the fullness of its cultural, social, and historical particularity in order that the world may know that the God of love has been revealed in Jesus Christ and that through him God is reconciling the world and announcing good news to all people."[62]

In other words, unity does not require uniformity.

Jesus said his Father's house has many rooms. In this metaphor, I like to imagine the Presbyterians hanging out in the library, the Baptists running the kitchen, the Anglicans setting the table, the Anabaptists washing feet with the hose in the backyard, the Lutherans making liturgy for the laundry, the Methodists stoking the fire in the hearth, the Catholics keeping the family history, the Pentecostals throwing open all the windows and doors to let more people in.

This is not to minimize the significance of our differences, of course. There are denominations of which I cannot in good conscience be a part because they ban women from the pulpit and gay and lesbian people from the table. Historically, churches have split over important issues like corruption, slavery, and civil rights. Doctrinal disputes may, in some cases, be negligible, but in others worth contesting. We're a family, after all, and so we fight like one.

Perhaps, when the Master Cobbler makes all things new, every good gift from each tradition will be melded together into one, all the impurities refined away. But in the meantime, our various traditions seem a sweet and necessary grace. And when we check our pride long enough to pay attention to the presence of the Spirit gusting across the globe, we catch glimpses of a God who defies our categories and expectations, a God who both inhabits and transcends our worship, art, theology, culture, experiences, and ideas.

For many, a confirmation ceremony marks the moment when they identify one of these Christian traditions as their own. I have not yet been confirmed, but I have taken joy in seeing friends and family find their way from one expression of the church to another, and in so doing, encounter their faith afresh, as if for the first time. I'm happy for my friend

Rachel who found in the Orthodox tradition a connection to the ancient, historic church that she missed growing up evangelical, and for Sarah, who found in the contemporary music of evangelical worship a passion and energy she missed being raised Anglican. I'm happy for Elizabeth, who found healing from her patriarchal, fundamentalist upbringing in connecting with Mary through the Catholic church, and for Robert, who found at a Presbyterian church in New York City the first intellectually rigorous engagement of his questions as an agnostic. None of these friends report perfect or painless experiences, even in their new church homes. As my friend Ed puts it: "When you join a church you're just picking which hot mess is your favorite." That sounds about right to me.

"Our lives are like islands in the sea," wrote William James, "or like trees in the forest. The maple and the pine may whisper to each other with their leaves . . . But the trees also commingle their roots in the darkness underground, and the islands also hang together through the ocean's bottom. Just so there is a continuum of cosmic consciousness, against which our individuality builds but accidental fences, and into which our several minds plunge as into a mother-sea or reservoir."[63]

Our differences matter, but ultimately, the boundaries we build between one another are but accidental fences in the endless continuum of God's grace. We are both a forest and a single tree—one big Trembling Giant, stirred by an invisible breeze.

TWENTY-SIX

Easter Doubt

I talk to God but the sky is empty.

—Sylvia Plath

IT WILL BOTHER YOU OFF AND ON, LIKE A ROCK IN YOUR shoe.

Or startle you, like the first crash of thunder in a summer storm.

Or lodge itself beneath your skin like a splinter.

Or show up again—the uninvited guest whose heavy footsteps you'd recognize anywhere, appearing at your front door with a suitcase in hand at the worst possible time.

Doubt will pull you farther out to sea like riptide.

Or hold your head under as you drown—triggered by an image, a question, something the pastor said, something that doesn't add up, the unlikelihood of it all, the too-good-to-be-trueness of it, the way the lady in the thick perfume behind you sings "Up from the grave he arose!" with more confidence in the single line of a song than you've managed to muster in the past two years.

Has it really been that long?

And you'll be sitting there in the dress you pulled out from the back of your closet, swallowing down the bread and wine, not believing a word of it.

Not a word.

So you'll fumble through those back-pocket prayers—*help me in my unbelief!*—while everyone around you moves on to verse two, verse three, verse four without you. You will feel their eyes on you, and you will recognize the concern behind their cheery greetings: "We haven't seen you here in a while! So good to have you back."

And you will know they are thinking exactly what you used to think about Easter Sunday Christians:

Nominal.
Lukewarm.
Indifferent.

But you won't know how to explain that there is nothing nominal or lukewarm or indifferent about standing in this hurricane of questions every day and staring each one down until you've mustered all the bravery and fortitude and trust it takes to whisper just one of them out loud on the car ride home:

"What if we made this up because we're afraid of death?"

And you won't know how to explain why, in that moment when the whisper rose out of your mouth like Jesus from the grave, you felt more alive and awake and resurrected than you have in ages because at least it was out, at least it was said, at least it wasn't buried in your chest anymore, clawing for freedom.

And, if you're lucky, someone in the car will recognize the bravery of the act. If you're lucky, there will be a moment of holy silence before someone wonders out loud if such a question might put a damper on Easter brunch.

But if you're not—if the question gets answered too quickly or if the silence goes on too long—please know you are not alone.

There are other people singing words to hymns they're not sure they believe today, other people digging out dresses from the backs of their closets today, other people ruining Easter brunch today, other people just showing up today.

And sometimes, just showing up, burial spices in hand, is all it takes to witness a miracle.

TWENTY-SEVEN

With God's Help

I come down to the water to cool my eyes. But
everywhere I look I see fire; that which isn't flint is
tinder, and the whole world sparks and flames.

—Annie Dillard

MY MOTHER ALWAYS SAID YOU DON'T HAVE TO BELIEVE
much to be an Episcopalian.

Indeed, when it comes to a unifying doctrine, the Anglican
tradition doesn't get too specific but defers to the central affir-
mations of the historic Christian creeds: that there is a good
and almighty God who is the creative force behind all things
seen and unseen; that this God is One, yet exists as three persons; that God loved the world enough to become flesh in the
person of Jesus Christ, who lived, taught, fed, healed, and suffered among us as both fully God and fully man; that Jesus was
conceived by the power of the Holy Spirit and born of a virgin; that Jesus was crucified on a Roman cross and buried in
the ground; that after three days dead, Jesus came back to life;

that Jesus ascended into heaven and reigns with God; that Jesus will return to bring justice and restoration; that God continues to work in the world through the Holy Spirit, the church, and God's people; that forgiveness is possible; that resurrection is possible; that eternal life is possible.

You know, *not much.*

For me, simply reciting the Apostles' Creed on a given Sunday means drawing from every last reserve of my faith, which is probably why I find the Episcopal Church both freeing and challenging in its elemental ecclesiology. And it's one of the reasons why, when Dan and I go to church these days, we make the thirty-mile drive to St. Luke's Episcopal Church, a bustling little congregation in the neighboring town of Cleveland, Tennessee. I like the liturgy, the lectionary, the centrality of the Eucharist in worship, *The Book of Common Prayer*, those giant red doors that are open to all. Dan likes the kind people and the fact that his wife doesn't come home from church angry anymore.

We aren't confirmed. We aren't even that plugged in. Right now, we're just showing up. And for whatever reason, the people of St. Luke's just keep loving us for showing up.

It took two years after the Mission folded for us to stagger back into semiregular church attendance. Our friends Chris and Tiffany found St. Luke's, one of the oldest congregations in the area, which meets in a lovely Oxford Movement American Gothic and has seen something of a resurgence of young families in recent years. Admired for its three-story bell tower, intricate interior woodwork, and beautiful stained-glass windows, the building was constructed in 1872 as a gift from the wealthy Craigmiles family in memory of their daughter, Nina, who was killed at age seven on St. Luke's Day when a train struck the horse and buggy carrying her. Throughout the church hide little tributes to Nina—an alcove behind the pulpit for her favorite flowers, her name etched into the corner of a stained-glass window. In the churchyard, next to the playground, stands a marble mausoleum, where the entire Craigmiles family is now buried. (The mysterious red-brown stain above the entrance has been the subject of local ghost stories for years.) Once a year, at Easter, the mausoleum is opened up, and the children of St. Luke's lead a processional from the church to lay a wreath of flowers on the grave. Life to death. Death to life.

Chris and Tiffany began attending shortly after we all dispersed from the Mission and, like the friend brave enough to test the depth of the swimming hole by jumping in first, took confirmation classes and reported back to us their experience. We visited on Easter and other holidays, always sitting in the back with easy egress to Lupi's Pizza down the street should we need to escape. But the rector, Father Joel, never told us what to think about evolution or how to vote in the next election, and once Dan learned about the method of *intinction*—whereby one dips the Eucharist wafer in the wine rather than drinking straight from the shared chalice—his germophobic concerns were assuaged. So we stayed.

In the spring of 2014, Chris and Tiffany invited us to attend their confirmation. The sacrament of confirmation takes a different shape depending on the tradition and circumstances of those receiving it, but in general, acknowledges the presence of the Holy Spirit in the baptized Christian's life and confirms his or her status as a beloved child of God in the family of the church. For those baptized as infants, confirmation provides an opportunity for them to affirm the tenets of the faith as adolescents or adults. For those new to a particular denomination or congregation, it serves as a sort of initiation rite, bestowing membership. The sacrament is typically conferred by a high-ranking church official, like a bishop, with an anointing, the laying on of hands, and prayer. *Catechism of the Catholic Church* captures the spirit of confirmation: "Recall that you have received the spiritual seal, the spirit of wisdom and under-standing, the spirit of right judgment and courage, the spirit of knowledge and reverence, the spirit of holy fear in God's presence. Guard what you have received. God the Father has marked you with his sign; Christ the Lord has confirmed you and placed his pledge, the Spirit, in your hearts."[64]

Confirmation day at St. Luke's meant breaking out the fold-ing metal chairs and cramming tighter in the pews, for the bishop was in town, conferring the rite at a single 10:45 a.m. service. We had to crane our necks to see Chris and Tiffany standing with about twenty other candidates near the front of the church, but found them easily once we spotted the bright hair bows of their two little girls, Early and Willa. Light streamed in through the stained glass, and as the chimes rang and the bishop joined the processional, a sense of excitement filled the room, the kids whispering about his tall hat and fancy staff, their parents gently shushing them.

I had thought the service would focus exclusively on the can-didates for confirmation, but like everything in the Episcopal Church, this event was participatory. After the candidates ver-bally reaffirmed their renunciation of evil and commitment to Jesus Christ, and after they had each been called by name and blessed by the bishop with his hands on their heads, the bishop turned to the congregation and asked us to stand.

"Will you who witness these vows do all in your power to support these persons in their life in Christ?"

"We will," came the chorused response.

I held in my mind Chris and Tiffany, Early and Willa, and little Walter on the way. What a beautiful life in Christ they had, and what a joyful task to support it.

"Let us join with those who are committing themselves to Christ and renew our own baptismal covenant," said the bishop, inviting all who were present to reaffirm their faith together.

"Do you believe in God the Father?" the bishop asked.

"I believe in God, the Father almighty, creator of heaven earth," I said, my voice joining Dan's, Chris and Tiffany's, Father Joel's, the East Tennessee accents surrounding us, and the voices of millions of Christians from around the world.

"Do you believe in Jesus Christ, the Son of God?"

"I believe in Jesus Christ, his only Son, our Lord," I said, falling into the familiar cadence of the Apostles' Creed. "He was conceived by the power of the Holy Spirit and born of the Virgin Mary. He suffered under Pontius Pilate, was crucified, died, and was buried. He descended to the dead. On the third day he rose again. He ascended into heaven, and is seated at the right hand of the Father. He will come again to judge the living and the dead."

"Do you believe in the Holy Spirit?"

"I believe in the Holy Spirit, the holy catholic Church, the communion of saints, the forgiveness of sins, the resurrection of the body, and the life everlasting."

"Will you continue in the apostles' teachings and fellowship, in the breaking of bread, and in the prayers?" the bishop asked.

"I will, with God's help," I said, swallowing hard.

"Will you preserve in resisting evil, and whenever you fall into sin, repent and return to the Lord?"

"I will, with God's help," I said. Tears clouded my eyes.

"Will you proclaim by word and example the Good News of God in Christ? Will you seek and serve Christ in all persons, loving your neighbor as yourself? Will you strive for justice and peace among all people, and respect the dignity of every human being?"

I will. I will. With God's help, I will.

In the silence that followed, it was as if all the amorphous vagaries of my faith coalesced into a single, tangible call: Repent. Break bread. Seek justice. Love neighbor. Christianity seemed at once the simplest and most impossible thing in the world. It seemed to me *confirmed*, sealed as the story of my life—that thing I'll never shake, that thing I'll always be.

In her memoir *Still*, Lauren Winner recounts the story of her friend Julian. When Julian was just twelve years old and preparing to be confirmed, she told her father—the pastor of the church—she wasn't sure she could go through with it. She wasn't sure she believed everything she was supposed to believe, at least not enough to make a promise before God and her congregation to believe those things forever.

He father told her, "What you promise when you are confirmed is not that you will believe this forever. What you promise when you are confirmed is that this is the story you will wrestle with forever."[65]

Mine is a stubborn and recalcitrant faith. It's all elbows and motion and kicked-up dust, like cartoon characters locked in a cloudy brawl. I'm still early in my journey, but I suspect it will go on like this for a while, perhaps until my last breath. The Episcopal Church is no less plagued by troubles than any other, but for now, it has given me the room to wrestle and it has reminded me what I'm wrestling for. And so, with God's help, I keep showing up.

TWENTY-EIGHT

Wind

The wind blows wherever it pleases. You hear its sound,
but you cannot tell where it comes from or where it
is going. So it is with everyone born of the Spirit.

—John 3:8

NICODEMUS CAME TO JESUS IN THE DEAD OF NIGHT. A
prominent member of the religious establishment, he had
questions for the radical rabbi who was making news around
Jerusalem, but feared for his own reputation should he be spotted in the company of a man who dined with sinners and who
had just made a big ol' scene overturning tables at the temple.

In art, the two are often depicted conversing on a flat roof-
top, stars above their heads, faces lit by lamplight. You can
almost hear the anxious hush in Nicodemus's voice as he con-
fesses, "We know you are a teacher who has come from God,
for no one could perform the signs you are doing if God were
not with him."

But . . .

Jesus wasn't playing by the rules. He was healing on the Sabbath, associating with lowlifes, criticizing the religious leaders. The incident at the temple had not gone over well with Nicodemus's friends.

Still, Nicodemus knew Scripture well enough to know God works through unexpected people: a seventy-four-year-old childless nomad, a criminal escaped from Egypt and afraid to speak, an impoverished Moabite woman, a shepherd too young to be king, a Persian concubine. He wasn't ready to discount Jesus just yet.

Jesus tells Nicodemus the Spirit is like a womb. To see the kingdom of God you need brand-new eyes. You must be born again.

Nicodemus doesn't understand.

Jesus says the Spirit is like water. To see God's work, you must be washed, renewed, reborn.

Still Nicodemus scratches his head.

Jesus says the Spirit is like wind. Employing a bit of wordplay, he uses the Greek word *pneuma*—which means both spirit and wind—and says the windy Spirit blows wherever it pleases. You can hear the windy Spirit, Jesus says, and you can even see its effects. But you don't know where it has come from and you don't get to tell it where to go. The windy Spirit just shows up. The same is true for people who have been reborn, for people who see the world with brand-new eyes. It's not because of their parents, or because of their status, or because of something they did, something they achieved. There's nothing on the outside, nothing physical that sets them apart. The windy Spirit just shows up and changes everything.

"You're supposed to be the expert!" Jesus cries. "Don't you know this already?"

This isn't something you can see with regular eyes, he says, and yet it's as plain as a hand right in front of your face if you know how to really *see*.

Nicodemus, it seems, eventually got it. He later defended Jesus when he was criticized by the religious leaders and, most notably, was near the cross when Jesus died. We tend to speak disparagingly of the Pharisees, lumping them together in a single group we've made synonymous with hypocrisy, and yet a Pharisee risked his reputation to speak up for his friend, a Pharisee stuck with Jesus after most of the disciples had run away, a Pharisee personally cared for Jesus' body when it had been all but abandoned by the world. Even a Pharisee, it seems, can be visited by the Spirit. Even a Pharisee can *see*.

This is what's most annoying and beautiful about the windy Spirit and why we so often miss it. It has this habit of showing up in all the wrong places and among all the wrong people, defying our categories and refusing to take direction. Nicodemus struggled to see the Spirit outside the religious institution. Today, some of us struggle to see the Spirit within the religious institution, often for good reason. But God is present both inside and outside the traditional church, working all sorts of everyday miracles to inspire and change us if only we *pay attention*.

"None of us can control what God does," says Sara Miles. "But we can open our eyes and see what God is doing."[66]

Sometimes I wonder how much I've missed because I haven't bothered to look, because I wrote off that church or that person or that denomination because I assumed God to be absent when there is not a corner of this world that God has abandoned.

We can't see the Spirit directly, but the apostle Paul said we will recognize its effects:

Love.
Joy.
Peace.
Patience.
Kindness.
Goodness.
Faithfulness.
Gentleness.
Self-control.

I saw *love* in the little church family that hosted, catered, and paid for the wedding of a young couple whose parents were not in the picture. I felt *joy* as I sang "Jesus Loves Me" with a chorus of kids orphaned by HIV/AIDS as our van tumbled through the bumpy streets of Hyderabad on our way to Sunday school. I witnessed *peace* when a Palestinian man and an Israeli woman, both of whom lost children to the conflict in their region, urged a room full of Christians to let their friendship be an example of looking for the humanity in one another. It was *patience* that brought the female minister to the bedside of the parishioner who vocally opposed her ordination but had no one else to visit him when he got sick.

I saw *kindness* in the man who, for many years, helped a special needs student at his school use the bathroom twice a day, but whose actions went uncelebrated until his funeral when the student himself gave testimony. It was *goodness* that inspired an online community to raise enough money to send a mother of eight diagnosed with stage-four pancreatic cancer on a weeklong beach vacation with her family.[67] I watched *faithfulness* when Brian Ward spent hours and hours preparing a sermon he would deliver to just five people. I felt *gentleness* in the hands that washed my feet in a moving initiation ceremony when I was an awkward freshman in college, anxious about starting over again. And I have admired, deeply, the *self-control* of my friends Justin, Matthew, Rachel, and Jeff who advocate for the acceptance of LGBT people in Christianity, often to harsh and cruel criticism, and yet continue to love and serve the very people who turned them out of the church, refusing to meet anger with anger or hate with hate.

The Spirit is like wind, like fire, like a bird, like a breath— moving through every language and every culture of this world, bursting out of every category and defying every metaphor.

Who's to say where She will travel next?

PART VI

Anointing of the Sick

TWENTY-NINE

Oil

You anoint my head with oil; my cup overflows.

—Psalm 23:5

To THE FREED SLAVES, GOD SMELLED LIKE CINNAMON, cassia, olive oil, and myrrh—sweet and earthy, nutty and warm. When Moses met God on Mount Sinai, God sent him back with a recipe for oil. This oil would anoint the temple, the altar, the religious furnishings, even the priests. No one else was to use that same perfume, God said. "Think of it as holy to me" (Exodus 30:22–38).

We know now what the Creator knew then: that the olfactory nerve is connected to the amygdala, the part of the brain associated with memory and emotion, which is why the fragrance of a particular flower or the scent of a certain soap can suddenly flood a body with a memory, stunning in its visceral clarity. God wanted his people to know his scent. He wanted them to remember.

And so the pages of Scripture positively drip with oil.

Nearly two hundred references speak of oil to light lamps, oil to soothe dry skin, oil to honor guests, oil to mark a sacred place, oil to solemnize a commitment, oil to entice, oil to comfort, oil to consecrate, oil to heal, oil to anoint priests, prophets, and kings, oil to prepare a body for burial.

To the ancient Israelites, prayer smelled like frankincense—balsamic, resinous, piney—said to be especially sweet to God's senses and thus continuously burned in the temple. Cleansing smelled like fresh hyssop, sex like cinnamon, saffron, and nard. Royalty smelled like myrrh—warm, pungent, and woody—an oil also used in burial and to celebrate weddings. Wealth smelled like thick, aromatic spikenard, temple sacrifice like hyssop and cedarwood.[68] For anointing, the prophets employed olive oil, perhaps with a touch of sweet cassia. To be anointed with oil was to be chosen, consecrated, and commissioned for a holy task. Messiah, or Christ, means "Anointed One."

"The Spirit of the Lord is on me," the Messiah said, "because he has anointed me to proclaim good news to the poor. He has sent me to proclaim freedom for the prisoners and recovery of sight for the blind, to set the oppressed free" (Luke 4:18).

"You have an anointing from the Holy One," said the apostle John to his fellow Christians "We are to God the pleasing aroma of Christ among those who are being saved," said the apostle Paul.[69]

The ancients knew, too, the healing properties of oils, which were applied to wounds and ingested as medicine. When James instructs the early church to anoint the sick with oil and to lay their hands on the sick and pray, the prescription is both practical and spiritually significant. The journey through suffering is a fraught and holy commission, one the Messiah himself knew well. Healing may come through medicine, through prayer, through presence and scent and calming touch, or through the consecrating of the journey as holy, dignified, and not without purpose or grace. The Catholic Church defines the anointing of the sick as "the conferral of a special grace on the Christian experiencing the difficulties inherent in the condition of grave illness or old age."[70] Even in death, the sick are anointed, reminded that the seal of the Holy Spirit is more permanent than the grave.

There is nothing magic about oil. It is merely a carrier—of memory, of healing, of grace. We anoint not to cure, but to heal. We anoint to soothe, to dignify, and even in our suffering, to remember the scent of God.

THIRTY

Healing

When we honestly ask ourselves which person in our lives
means the most to us, we often find that it is those who, instead
of giving advice, solutions, or cures, have chosen rather to share
our pain and touch our wounds with a warm and tender hand.

—Henri Nouwen

CLAIRE LOVED HER BUSY, METROPOLITAN CHURCH.[71] IT
was where she connected with her best friends, where she met
her husband, where she supported and served a homeless ministry, where she fit. When her husband secured a job on the
church staff and Claire learned she was pregnant, life seemed
to be falling into place.

"Two months before the baby was born, our house flooded
and we had to move out," Claire wrote in her e-mail to me.
"One month before the baby was born, my parked car was hit
and was rendered inoperable. One day before the baby was
born, he stopped moving.

"I didn't know that healthy, full-term babies could be born

stillborn," she said. "I went to the hospital with hope and fear. They never found a heartbeat."

The church rallied, helping with funeral costs and meals, even providing a cabin for a weekend getaway for Claire and her husband. But when the couple returned to face down the long and arduous journey through grief, they found themselves alone.

"There are no worship songs for those mourning a traumatic death," Claire wrote. "There is no testimony about feeling forsaken when God does not intervene to save a baby. We wanted so desperately for our church and pastor to struggle with us, to question, to face this ugly, brutal truth." But Claire's agony was met largely by platitudes—Bible verses, theological answers, promises of better days ahead.

Claire found healing outside the church walls—in counseling, among a couple of close friends, on Internet forums where faith, doubt, and grief were discussed openly. Eventually she and her husband connected to another church, but Claire still finds herself struggling to worship at times.

"My counselor says that being part of a church in the midst of grief can be like having ten thousand antennae," she said. "Anything and everything hurts."

I get a lot of e-mails from people like Claire, people who fit right into the church *until* . . .

the divorce.
the diagnosis.
the miscarriage.
the depression.
someone comes out.
someone asks a question.
an uncomfortable truth is spoken out loud.

And what they find is when they bring their pain or their doubt or their uncomfortable truth to church, someone immediately grabs it out of their hands to try and fix it, to try and make it go away. Bible verses are quoted. Assurances are given. Plans with ten steps and measurable results are made. With good intentions tinged with fear, Christians scour their inventory for a cure.

But there is a difference between curing and healing, and I believe the church is called to the slow and difficult work of healing. We are called to enter into one another's pain, anoint it as holy, and stick around no matter the outcome.

In her book *Jesus Freak*, Sara Miles explains it like this: "Jesus calls his disciples, giving us authority to heal and sending us out. He doesn't show us how to reliably cure a molar pregnancy. He doesn't show us how to make a blind man see, dry every tear, or even drive out all kinds of demons. But he shows us how to enter into a way of life in which the broken and sick pieces are held in love, and given meaning. In which strangers literally touch each other, and in doing so make a community spacious enough for everyone."[72]

The thing about healing, as opposed to curing, is that it is relational. It takes time. It is inefficient, like a meandering river. Rarely does healing follow a straight or well-lit path. Rarely does it conform to our expectations or resolve in a timely manner. Walking with someone through grief, or through the process of reconciliation, requires patience, presence, and a willingness to wander, to take the scenic route.

But the modern-day church doesn't like to wander or wait. The modern-day church likes *results*. Convinced the gospel is a product we've got to sell to an increasingly shrinking market, we like our people to function as walking advertisements: happy, put-together, finished—proof that this Jesus stuff

WORKS! At its best, such a culture generates pews of *Stepford Wife*–style robots with painted smiles and programmed moves. At its worst, it creates environments where abuse and corruption get covered up to protect reputations and preserve image. "The world is watching," Christians like to say, "so let's be on our best behavior and quickly hide the mess. Let's throw up some before-and-after shots and roll that flashy footage of our miracle product blanching out every sign of dirt, hiding every sign of disease."

But if the world is watching, we might as well tell the truth. And the truth is, the church doesn't offer a cure. It doesn't offer a quick fix. The church offers death and resurrection. The church offers the messy, inconvenient, gut-wrenching, never-ending work of healing and reconciliation. The church offers *grace*.

Anything else we try to peddle is snake oil. It's not the real thing.

As Brené Brown puts it, "I went to church thinking it would be like an epidural, that it would take the pain away . . . But church isn't like an epidural; it's like a midwife . . . I thought faith would say, 'I'll take away the pain and discomfort, but what it ended up saying was, 'I'll sit with you in it.'"[73]

I know a faith healer here in Tennessee who understands this better than most. Becca Stevens is an Episcopal priest from Nashville and the founder of Thistle Farms, a social enterprise that trains and employs women recovering from abuse, prostitution, addiction, sex trafficking, imprisonment, and life on the streets. As the women heal through the therapy and community offered by the Magdalene program, they offer healing to others through the aromatic bath and body products they make from essential oils and sell in stores and online.[74] At Thistle Farms, healing smells like lavender, tea tree, peppermint, and vanilla. It feels like lotion and body balm massaged into the skin. It looks like a flickering candle, and sounds like the whistle of a teapot singing from the new Thistle Stop Café. And it takes time.

"In making and selling oils," Becca writes, "we are each reminded that healing is not an event, but rather a journey we walk as we make our way back to the memory of God."[75]

That journey isn't always a smooth one. Although 72 percent of women who join Magdalene are clean and sober two and a half years after beginning the program, like any other recovery group, this one knows the sting of disappointment, failure, wrong turns, and relapse. But love, Becca says, "carries us beyond the narrow path of believing that healing is moving from diagnosing to cure . . . Healing is a natural outcome of love. As we learn how to love, we learn how to heal."[76]

In addition to her work at Thistle Farms, Becca advocates for creative and effusive use of healing oils in churches—not as a panacea or magic charm, but as a gift, an outward sign of inward grace. Why settle for just a drop of oil for chrism, she argues, when you can fill an entire sanctuary with sweet aroma and engage all the senses in worship? At her own church, a table set with a variety of essential oils—lavender, cinnamon leaf, lemongrass, jasmine, geranium, balsam, myrrh—invites parishioners to make their own blends for anointing the hands and feet of the people they love and serve. Becca concocts special blends for expectant mothers, couples in premarital counseling, those who are sick, those embarking on exciting new journeys, and those traveling difficult roads of healing. The scent, combined with a prayer and gentle touch, can have a powerful healing effect on a person, physically, spiritually, and emotionally. And the time and intention it takes to create a custom scent signals a commitment to stick around for the long haul.

Ultimately, an anointing is an acknowledgment. It's a way to speak to someone who is suffering, and without words or platitudes or empty solutions, say, *this is a big deal, this matters, I'm here.* In a world of cure-alls and quick fixes, true healing may be one of the most powerful and countercultural gifts the church has to offer the world, if only we surrender our impulse to cure, if only we let love do its slow, meandering work.

....

Seven years after the "Vote Yes On One" campaign sent me flee-ing from the church, I discovered church again in an unlikely place: the Gay Christian Network's annual "Live It Out" con-ference in Chicago.

Founded by Justin Lee, a young gay man who grew up Southern Baptist and survived the destructive effects of "ex-gay ministries" to eventually accept and embrace his sexuality, the Gay Christian Network offers community and support to gay, lesbian, bisexual, and transgender Christians, along with their friends, family, and allies. The group is ecumenical, but attracts a lot of evangelicals, many of whom have been mar-ginalized or kicked out of the churches in which they grew up. Some of the more than seven hundred attendees believed Scripture compelled them to commit their lives to celibacy while others believed Scripture granted them the freedom to pursue same-sex relationships and marriage. There was room at the table for all.

I spoke at the conference as an ally, but within hours of arriving at the Westin on the Chicago River, it became clear I had little to teach these brothers and sisters in Christ and everything to learn from them. I speak at dozens of Christian conferences in a given year, but I've never participated in one so energized by the Spirit, so devoid of empty showmanship, so grounded in love and abounding in grace. As one attendee put it, "this is an unapologetically Christian conference."

Indeed it was. There was communion, confession, worship, and fellowship. There was deep concern for honoring Scripture and loving as Christ would love, even through differences and pain. There was lots of hugging and crying and praying . . . and argyle.

But what startled me the most was the degree to which so many attendees had suffered, sometimes brutally, at the hands of Christians trying to "cure" them of their sexual orientation. One young woman described undergoing an exorcism ceremony designed to cast the demon of lesbianism from her body. Another went to counseling where her Christian therapist insisted she must have been molested or mistreated by her parents when she hadn't. One man followed the advice of his pastor and married a woman, hoping heterosexual sex would make him straight, a decision that led to heartbreaking consequences. Many at the conference had gone through evangelical ex-gay ministries, the largest of which had recently shut its doors when its president admitted that reparative therapy to change sexual orientation is rarely, if ever, effective. Person after person told stories about getting kicked out of their church or their family upon coming out. (Of the estimated 1.6 million homeless American youth, between 20 and 40 percent identify as lesbian, gay, bisexual, or transgender.) Far too many described contemplating suicide as teenagers after begging God to "fix" them to no avail.

And yet here they were, when they had every right in the world to run as far away from the church as their legs would carry them, worshipping together, praying together, healing together. Here they were, *being* the church that had rejected them. I felt simultaneously furious at Christianity's enormous capacity to wound and awed by its miraculous capacity to heal.

The final night of the conference was set aside for an open mic, in which participants were invited to share their stories in front of the whole group in the main ballroom. One by one, hundreds of brave men and women approached the microphone, took a deep breath, and told the truth.

"I'm Mary and I'm Jacob's mom," said a short woman with a midwestern accent who wore jeans, a white T-shirt and, like several of the parents at the conference, a giant button pin that announced "FREE MOM HUGS" in tall red letters.[77]

"Tonight I want to ask Jacob's forgiveness, and your forgiveness too, because . . ." Her voice began to tremble. "Because until this weekend I was ashamed of my son."

She stifled a sob with her hands while we waited in a thick silence.

"I didn't want the people at my church to know he was gay because I was afraid of what they would think, what they might say," she finally said. "But not anymore. I'm so proud of my beautiful son, and of all of you. I'm so proud that I'm going to shout it from the rooftops!"

A gentle laugh rippled through the room.

"I'm so sorry," Mary said, first looking to her son on the front row and then to the rest of the audience. "I'm so very sorry. Please forgive me."

"We forgive you!" shouted a woman behind me.

Jacob ran to front of the room and embraced his mom. They held each other for a few minutes before the next person approached the mic.

"I remember the first time I was called a . . . homophobic word," said a young woman, no more than twenty, who wore a flower in her hair and kept her eyes on her shoes. It took her a few moments to form the next words.

"It was at church."

Around the room, people hummed in sad ascent.

"This is the first time in a long time I've been able to be around Christians without totally freaking out," she said, without ever looking up. "So thanks for that."

"From the time I was a teenager, I've started every day the exact same way," said a handsome man who wore a fedora and spoke with confidence.

"First, I look in the mirror and ask myself, 'Does this outfit look too gay?'"

The crowd chuckled.

"After I've *changed*," he said with a wry laugh, "I go back to the mirror and say to myself, 'Mike, watch your hands. Mike, be careful with your voice. Mike, don't laugh too loud. Mike, don't walk that way. Mike, whatever you do, *don't act so gay*.'"

His voice suddenly cracked.

"I didn't want to lose my job in ministry," he said, after collecting himself. "But I'm so tired of that routine. After twenty years, I can't keep doing that. I'm done. I'm done pretending. I'm done faking it. It's time to tell the truth: I'm a Christian and I'm gay."

The crowd applauded.

An African American man in a wheelchair followed and brought the house down when he approached the mic, waited a moment, and declared, "I'm black. I'm disabled. I'm gay. And I live in Mississippi. *What was God thinking?*"

He was followed by a college student who said he finally worked up the courage to come out to his parents.

"It didn't go as well as I'd hoped," he said. And in the painful silence that followed far too many understood.

And then there was the young man who had attended the year before in the midst of a deep depression, but who had returned this year with a new church, a healthier family dynamic, and a boyfriend. "It gets better," he said.

Near the end of the session, a slight, middle-aged man in a dress shirt approached the microphone.

"I'm here to ask your forgiveness," he said quietly.

"I've been a pastor with a conservative denomination for more than thirty years, and I used to be an antigay apologist. I knew every argument, every Bible verse, every angle, and every position. I could win a debate with just about anyone, and I confess I yelled down more than a few 'heretics' in my time. I was absolutely certain that what I was saying was true and I assumed I'd defend that truth to death. But then I met a young lesbian woman who, over a period of many years, slowly changed my mind. She is a person of great faith and grace, and her life was her greatest apologetic."

The man began to sob into his hands.

"I'm so sorry for what I did to you," he finally continued. "I might not have hurt any of you directly, but I know my misguided apologetics, and then my silent complicity, probably did more damage than I can ever know. I am truly sorry and I humbly repent of my actions. Please forgive me."

"We forgive you!" someone shouted from up front.

But the pastor held up his hand and then continued to speak.

"And if things couldn't get any weirder," he said with a nervous laugh, "I was dropping my son off at school the other day—he's a senior in high school—and we started talking about this very issue. When I told him that I'd recently changed my mind about homosexuality, he got really quiet for a minute and then he said, 'Dad, I'm gay.'"

Nearly everyone in the room gasped.

"Sometimes I wonder if these last few years of studying, praying, and rethinking things were all to prepare me for that very moment," the pastor said, his voice quivering. "It was one of the most important moments of my life. I'm so glad I was ready. I'm so glad I was ready to love my son for who he is."

By the end of the open mic session, I understood exactly why they say not to bother with mascara at this thing. It was two of the most healing, powerful, grace-drenched hours of my life. It was, at last, church.

I had a conversation with someone the other day who said he wondered if perhaps LGBT Christians had a special role to play in teaching the church how to more thoughtfully engage issues surrounding gender and sexuality. I told him I didn't think that went far enough, that ever since the Gay Christian Network conference, I've been convinced that LGBT Christians have a special role to play in teaching the church how to be *Christian*.

Christians who tell each other the truth.

Christians who confess our sins and forgive our enemies.

Christians who embrace our neighbors.

Christians who sit together in our pain, and in our healing, and wait for resurrection.

....

Sometimes people ask me if I believe in faith healings.

What I think they're asking is if I believe a pastor can lay hands on a man and cure him of alcoholism, or if a religious shrine possesses the power to coax the paralyzed out of their wheelchairs, or if rallying around a little girl with twenty-four hours of prayer can reverse the progression of her cancer.

I don't know. I've watched too many people of strong faith succumb to illness and tragedy to believe God shows any sort of favoritism in these matters. (And yet, inexplicably, I always pray.)

So when I'm asked about faith healings, I tell people about Thistle Farms. I tell them about the Gay Christian Network. I tell them about the widows I met in India who haven't been cured of their HIV but who are healing from their poverty and hopelessness by loving one another well. I tell them about the Epic Fail Pastors Conference, and the abuse survivors I've met through the blog. I tell them about my own journey away from and back to church. Then I shrug my shoulders and say, "I suppose anything's possible."

THIRTY-ONE

Evangelical Acedia

*And I know all the steps up to your door. But
I don't wanna go there anymore.*

—Taylor Swift

"SEEMS TO ME THAT FOR YOU, EVANGELICALISM IS LIKE
the boyfriend you broke up with two years ago but whose
Facebook page you still check compulsively."

Well, that was it in a nutshell, wasn't it? And coming from
a Baptist preacher of all people.

He'd arrived at the hotel in his giant SUV a good fifteen
minutes earlier to pick me up for a speaking gig at Wingate
University near Charlotte, but I'd made him wait so I could
calm down, wash my face with cold water, and put on some
makeup. I couldn't remember the last time I'd cried so hard.

It all started when World Vision, a humanitarian organization I had long supported and even traveled with, announced a
change to its hiring policy allowing people in same-sex marriages
to work in its US offices. In response, conservative evangelicals

rallied in protest, and within seventy-two hours, more than ten thousand children had lost their financial support from cancelled World Vision sponsorships.

Ten thousand children.

To try and stem some of the bleeding, I joined with several other World Vision bloggers to encourage my readers to sponsor children or make one-time donations to the organization, which was reeling as church after church called to cut off funding. We had raised several thousand dollars and multiple sponsorships when the CEO of World Vision announced the charity would reverse its decision and return to its old policy against gay and lesbian employees.

It had worked. Using needy kids as bargaining chips in the culture war had actually worked.

According to the CEO, within hours of the change, phone calls flooded the offices with people asking, "Can I have my child back?"[78]

News of the reversal reached me by social media minutes before I was to be picked up to speak at Wingate. I suppose you could call it a punch to the gut, but the breathlessness with which the incident left me is more akin to chronic pain than a single injury from which one can fully heal. It still hurts.

The Baptist preacher was mad about it, too, and in his North Carolina drawl ranted all the way from the hotel to campus, which made me feel better. But having been raised in the more progressive stream of the Baptist tradition, he viewed the situation as something of an outsider, an observer of the infighting rather than a participant in it. He could safely roll his eyes and sigh, as one might while watching political pundits shout at each other on TV, without feeling a deep sense of personal investment or loss. I envied him for it.

Then he asked me why, despite attending an Episcopal

church and holding more progressive views, I still engaged in the evangelical conversation, online and in my books. And for about the hundredth in my life, I blustered and fulminated and declared with impassioned, self-important resolve that this was the final straw and I was finished with evangelicalism once and for all. "That's it!" I said. "I'm done!" I cried, before picking up my phone to tweet all about it.

That's when the Baptist pastor said the thing about Facebook.

The last time I'd been this angry at evangelicalism was a few years before, when Dan and I were invited into the home of some local churchgoers for what they deemed "a conversation about your faith experience," but which turned out to be a classic evangelical intervention. We squirmed uncomfortably on the couch, a plate of fresh chocolate chip cookies on the cushion between us, as four people we barely knew—an older couple that was friends of my family and a younger couple we'd never met until that night—expressed deep concern for our spiritual health given our acceptance of evolution and women's ordination. When the conversation turned to same-sex marriage, the older man's face gnarled and reddened, and Dan and I made an excuse to leave early. The minute we shut the doors of the Acclaim I vowed never to entangle myself with "those evangelicals" again. "That's it!" I said. "I'm done!"

Every time this happens, the big breakup is followed by a month or two of complete religious lassitude, in which I grow indifferent to prayer, indifferent to Scripture, indifferent to the very sort of theological discourse that used to invigorate and challenge me. Some evangelical pastor somewhere writes an article about how yoga pants incite the incontrollable lusts of men, and I can't generate the energy to debate Matthew 5:29 with him even though there are a dozen e-mails in my in-box asking me to respond. "Not my circus, not my monkeys," I say.

People invite us out, but I stay in. Sunday morning rolls around and I pull the covers over my head. I sink into a mild depression, a religious acedia, and I give my cynicism free reign. When a reporter working on a story about Christian feminism asks, "Would you like us to identify you as an evangelical?" I blow a bunch of air through my nose and say, "Hell if I know."

All I want is to be rid of this *investment*, this notion that I've got some sort of stake in the future of American evangelicalism when it's clear American evangelicalism doesn't want me anymore. If I can just stop caring, I imagine, the disappointment won't hurt as much. If I just give up, I will finally be free.

And then I get a letter in the mailbox from a sixty-year-old woman who has decided to pursue her lifelong dream of ordination thanks to a conversation she found on the blog. And then our evangelical neighbors invite Dan over for dinner while I'm out of town. And then I have a great conversation with my parents about the Gay Christian Network. And then the latest Scot McKnight book arrives on the doorstep. And then I take communion.

And suddenly I'm caring again. I'm *invested* again. I realize I can no more break up with my religious heritage than I can with my parents. I may not worship in an evangelical church anymore or even embrace evangelical theology, but as long as I have an investment in the church universal, I have an investment in the community that first introduced me to Jesus. Like it or not, I've got skin in the game.

And then they make an American Heritage Bible and we're back to breaking up again. So basically my relationship with evangelicalism is like a Taylor Swift song set to repeat.

The World Vision incident sent me into as deep a religious depression as I've ever known, and I'm still struggling to climb out of it. I know a lot of people who walked away from evangelicalism for good when they saw what happened, and I know a few who walked away from the entire church, unable to reconcile the love they see in Jesus with the condemnation they hear from his followers. But what I'm learning this time around, as I process my frustration and disappointment and as I catch those first ribbons of dawn's light on the horizon, is that I can't begin to heal until I've acknowledged my pain, and I can't acknowledge my pain until I've kicked my dependence on cynicism.

Cynicism is a powerful anesthetic we use to numb ourselves to pain, but which also, by its nature, numbs us to truth and joy. Grief is healthy. Even anger can be healthy. But numbing ourselves with cynicism in an effort to avoid feeling those things is not.

When I write off all evangelicals as hateful and ignorant, I am numbing myself with cynicism. When I jeer at their foibles, I am numbing myself with cynicism. When I roll my eyes and fold my arms and say, "Well, I know God can't be present over *there*," I am numbing myself with cynicism.

And I am missing out. I am missing out on a God who surprises us by showing up where we don't think God belongs. I am missing out on a God whose grace I need just as desperately, just as innately as the lady who dropped her child sponsorship in a protest against gay marriage. Cynicism may help us create simpler storylines with good guys and bad guys, but it doesn't make us any better at telling the truth, which is that most of us are a frightening mix of good and evil, sinner and saint.

The annoying thing about being human is that to be fully engaged with the world, we must be vulnerable. And the annoying thing about being vulnerable is that sometimes it means we get hurt. And when your family includes the universal church, you're going to get hurt. Probably more than once.

This doesn't mean we stay in unhealthy churches or allow abusive people to continue to abuse. It doesn't mean we participate in congregations that sap us of our life or make us fight to belong. It just means that if we want to heal from our wounds, including those we receive from the church, we have to kick the cynicism habit first. We have to allow ourselves to feel the pain and joy and heartache of being in relationship with other human beings. In the end, it's the only way to really live, even if it means staying *invested*, even if it means taking a risk and losing it all.

THIRTY-TWO

This Whole Business With the Hearse

The report of my death was an exaggeration.

—Mark Twain

In 2013, a megachurch pastor famous for his controversial antics arrived to a Sunday evening worship service at his church in Seattle in a long black hearse. Dressed in formal funeral attire, he posed for waiting photographers before going inside and preaching a sermon about how the church in America is dying and it's up to Christians to revive it. A few weeks later, his book *A Call to Resurgence: Will Christianity Have a Funeral or a Future?* hit the shelves, complete with a hearse in sepia tones gracing the cover.

It has become popular in recent years for Christians to speak of the impending death of the church. Conversations at denominational meetings and Christian conferences are as sotto voce as conversations around the dinner table about how this may be Aunt Marie's last Christmas so we might as well let the racist comment slide. The alarm is not completely unfounded. Polls show the percentage of self-identified Christians in the United States has fallen from 86 percent to 76 percent since 1990, while the percentage of people claiming no religious affiliation has doubled, rising to 16 percent.[79] Young adults seem especially disinterested in faith, with nearly three out of every five young Christians disconnecting from church life after age fifteen.[80]

I confess to citing these numbers ominously myself from time to time, especially when I want to make a point about how millennials are losing faith in the church over issues related to politics, sexuality, science, and social justice. I may have uttered something along the lines of "adapt or die" in my writing once or twice. I may have jumped the gun and administered last rites.

But lately I've been wondering if a little death and resurrection might be just what church needs right now, if maybe all this talk of waning numbers and shrinking influence means our empire-building days are over, and if maybe that's a good thing.

Death is something empires worry about, not something gardeners worry about. It's certainly not something resurrection people worry about.

G. K. Chesterton put it this way: "Christendom has had a series of revolutions, and in each one of them Christianity has died. Christianity has died many times and risen again; for it had a God who knew the way out of the grave."[81]

I don't know exactly what this new revolution will look like, but as the center of Christianity shifts from the global West to the global South and East, and as Christians in the United States are forced to gauge the success of the church by something other than money and power, I hope it looks like altars transforming into tables, gates transforming into open doors, and cure-alls transforming into healing oils. I hope it looks like a kingdom that belongs not to the rich, but to the poor, not to the triumphant but to the meek, not to the culture warriors but to the peacemakers. If Christianity must die, may it die to the old way of dominance and control and be resurrected to the Way of Jesus, the Way of the cross.

I recently heard a story about a United Methodist church that was in decline. Once a thriving congregation in east Durham, North Carolina, membership had dwindled to about forty people who struggled to maintain the beautiful old church building on their own. A new pastor, fresh out of divinity school, tried her best to swoop in and fix things by resurrecting the finance committee, consolidating accounts, selling all the unused church vans, and raising payment on the rented parsonage, but the church only managed to limp along. It wasn't until several other congregations from the neighborhood approached the church about meeting in their building that things began to change.

A nondenominational African American church worshiped in the sanctuary on Sunday evenings and provided monthly offerings to cover utilities. A Baptist church asked for space to teach English as a Second Language to the Spanish-speaking residents of the neighborhood. And then, a Methodist church-start of immigrants from Zimbabwe asked to use their building for worship at eleven a.m.—the same time the original congregation usually met. For the next year, the original congregation worshipped in the second-floor sanctuary, while the church-start worshipped in a room below, and in their native language—Shona. The pastor said her sermons were often punctuated by the beating of African drums.

The two churches shared meals together and held several joint worship services, including a Christmas Eve service with "Silent Night" sung in both English and Shona. But while the immigrant church-start continued to grow and grow, the original congregation continued to shrink and shrink, as its aging members died or moved away.

"Clearly it made no sense for a thriving congregation to be squashed in their worship space while thirty people knocked around upstairs in a sanctuary built for five hundred," the pastor explained. The dwindling congregation, she said, was "stuck somewhere between life and death."

So the church entered a period of praying and discernment, and time and again they returned to Mark 8:34–35: "If any want to become my followers, let them deny themselves and take up their cross and follow me. For those who want to save their life will lose it, and those who lose their life for my sake, and for the sake of the gospel, will save it" (NRSV).

Together, the church voted to give everything—building, furnishings, parsonage—to the Zimbabwean church-plant. The congregation itself stuck together and eventually dovetailed into another community that invited the few remaining members to worship in their space.

It was a kind of death, certainly. But, as the pastor puts it, "it was good death."[82]

I heard another moving story, this one from a woman I met at the Gay Christian Network. Like so many, Stacey grew up evangelical and loved every minute of church life until she realized she was gay. Suddenly, she said, "What was once my sanctuary became a dark and scary place." Stacey was told she had to choose between God and her sexuality. After years of begging God to make her straight, Stacey finally accepted that the God who knit her together in her mother's womb loved her unconditionally, sexuality and all.

When Stacey and her wife, Tams, moved to Vancouver, British Columbia, in 2010, they searched for an evangelical church. Most of the pastors they queried explained that while the couple was welcome to participate in worship, they would be prohibited from serving in any of the church's ministries, which was a priority to Stacey and Tams. Finally, they found the Cove, a small evangelical church with both conservative and progressive membership and a pastor committed to welcoming all. Even though they were the only gay couple in the church, Stacey and Tams fit right in and were embraced by the community. They joined a small group, got involved in Bible study, and before long were serving on the worship team and in the children's ministry. Stacey said the church reminded her of what Jesus said in John 13:35: "By this everyone will know that you are my disciples, if you love one another."

Eventually, Stacey and her wife became members of the ten-year-old church, a move that caught the attention of the denomination with which it was affiliated. A representative from the denomination came to investigate, as membership for LGBT people was prohibited by the larger church body.

"There it was," Stacey wrote in a guest post for my blog. "We knew it was coming. The spotlight had zeroed in on us once again. We had heard so many stories of our gay friends getting kicked out of their churches, or being asked to step down from ministry, or just being ignored by everyone until they left." Stacey feared they would be next and she would have to relive all the pain and rejection from her previous church experience.

But the Cove was different. The church refused to cast Stacey and her wife out. Their pastor met with denominational leaders several times to try and smooth things over, but in 2013 the church received a letter from the denomination announcing it would pull all of its funding from the Cove, effectively disbanding the small congregation.

"On Sunday, May 26, 2013, Cove had its last gathering together," wrote Stacey. "In a way, it felt like a funeral, but also a celebration. Our pastor had always challenged us to be a church to our communities outside of these walls, and now was our chance. We shared one last time, took up a collection for our pastor and his family, and then gathered in a huge circle to ask God to use this for His glory. My heart was so sad, and yet, so incredibly full."

"I always thought to myself, 'This place is too good to be true,'" Stacey said, "and maybe it was. Or maybe it was the start of a movement, a movement to embrace love over legalism, regardless of the cost. After all, isn't that what Christ came to teach us?"

It was a death, but it was a good death.[83]

As the shape of Christianity changes and our churches adapt to a new world, we have a choice: we can drive our hearses around bemoaning every augur of death, or we can trust that the same God who raised Jesus from the dead is busy making something new. As long as Christians are breaking the bread and pouring the wine, as long as we are healing the sick and baptizing sinners, as long as we are preaching the Word and paying attention, the church lives, and Jesus said even the gates of hell cannot prevail against it. We might as well trust him, since he knows a thing or two about the way out of the grave.

"New life starts in the dark," writes Barbara Brown Taylor. "Whether it is a seed in the ground, a baby in the womb, or Jesus in the tomb, it starts in the dark."[84]

THIRTY-THREE

Perfume

Smell is a potent wizard that transports you across
thousands of miles and all the years you have lived.

—Helen Keller

WHEN REFERRING TO THE EARLIEST FOLLOWERS OF
Jesus, the Gospel writers often speak of two groups of disciples:
the Twelve and the Women. The Twelve are the dozen Jewish
men chosen by Jesus to be his closest companions and first
apostles, symbolic of the twelve tribes of Israel. The Women
refer to an unspecified number of female disciples who also
followed Jesus, welcoming him into their homes, financing his
ministry, learning from him as their rabbi, and teaching the
Twelve through their acts of faithfulness. While the Women
appear throughout the Gospels, they feature most prominently
in the stories of Jesus' Passion—his last meals, his arrest and
trial, his death, and his resurrection—because when nearly
everyone else abandoned Jesus in fear and disappointment, the
women stuck around.

Just days before his betrayal, Jesus and his disciples were eating at the home of Simon the leper in Bethany. While they reclined at the table, a woman John identifies as Mary of Bethany approached Jesus with an alabaster jar of expensive perfume, worth about a year's wages. Mary broke the jar of spikenard, pouring the perfume on Jesus' body. The house filled with its pungent, woody fragrance as she anointed Jesus' head and feet, even daring to wipe his skin with her hair.

Everything about the incident was offensive—an interrupted meal, an excessive gift, a woman daring to touch a man *with her hair*. It was also highly symbolic. In Jesus' culture, the act of anointing signified selection for a special role or task. The heads of kings were anointed with oil as part of their coronation ceremony, often by a religious leader, and so this woman finds herself in the untraditional position of prophet and priest, anointing the Messiah. In the upside-down kingdom of Jesus, it makes perfect sense.

Anointing the head is one thing, but anointing the feet is another. Anointing the feet models the very service, discipleship, and love Jesus taught. In a culture in which a woman's touch was often forbidden, Mary dares to cradle the feet of Jesus in her hands and spread the oil across his ankles and toes with the ends of her hair. Rather than measuring out a small amount of oil, Mary breaks the jar and lets it all pour out. She's all-in, fully committed, sparing no expense. The oil she may have been reserving for her own burial, or the burial of a loved one, has been poured out generously, without thought of the future. The humility of her action foreshadows the foot washing that is to come, when Jesus washes his disciples' feet.

But in the midst of all this symbolism and foreshadowing, Jesus sees something else at work. He interprets the woman's act of worship as preparation for his burial. When the disciples rebuke the woman for what they see as a waste of money, Jesus responds by saying, "Let her alone; why do you trouble her? She has performed a good service for me. For you always have the poor with you, and you can show kindness to them whenever you wish; but you will not always have me. She has done what she could; she has anointed my body beforehand for its burial" (Mark 14:6–8 NRSV).

Jesus had been speaking of his impending death for a while, but the Twelve were having none of it. When Jesus told Peter that "the Messiah must be rejected, suffer, and die; then he will be raised," Peter responded with such an impassioned protest that Jesus rebuked him with "get behind me, Satan!" In another instance, Jesus spoke ominously of his death and the disciples respond by debating who would be the greatest in the coming kingdom. And in another, James and John miss the point entirely by responding to Jesus' prediction with requests to sit at his right and left hands.

Clearly, the Twelve struggled to conceive of a kingdom that would begin not with the death of their enemies, but with the death of their friend at the hands of their enemies. I suspect this is why they complained about the "waste" of money exhibited by the anointing. They imagined that their ministry with Jesus would continue for months and years to come. You can sense the sadness in Jesus' words when he reminds them, yet again, that he will not always be with them, that he is preparing for the most difficult days of his life.

We cannot know for sure whether Mary saw her actions as a prelude to her teacher's upcoming death and burial. I suspect she knew instinctively, the way women know these things, that a man who dines at a sick man's house, who allows a woman to touch him with her hair, who rebukes Pharisees and befriends prostitutes, would not survive for long in the world in which she lived. Surely a woman in this society would understand it better than a man. The marginalized are always the first to comprehend death and resurrection.

Perhaps this is why the women stayed by Jesus' side through his death and burial, after so many of the Twelve betrayed him, denied him, and fled from him in fear. This was the course of things, the women knew. They would see it through to the end because Jesus was their friend, and friends love one another even through pain, even through death. For their faithful friendship, the women are rewarded with being the first to witness the resurrection of Christ, the first to preach the gospel of the risen Lord.

For her act of worship Jesus praises Mary in unparalleled terms. "Truly I tell you, wherever the good news is proclaimed in the whole world, what she has done will be told in remembrance of her" (Mark 14:9 NRSV).

What a remarkable thought—that at every communion, every Easter service, every cathedral and every tent revival, from Israel to Africa, to Europe to China, this woman's story should be on our lips, right along with Christ's.

And yet, while we break the bread and drink the wine, we rarely pour out enough oil to fill a room with its fragrance. We rarely indulge all of our senses in an act of pure, impractical worship. Jesus wanted us to remember, but we have forgotten.

Perhaps we should bring back this oil, this costly perfume, and make it part of our Eucharist. Perhaps, with the help of the Spirit, the scent of it might trigger our collective memory.

PART VII

Marriage

THIRTY-FOUR

Crowns

*They will enter Zion with singing; everlasting joy will
crown their heads. Gladness and joy will overtake
them, and sorrow and sighing will flee away.*

—Isaiah 35:10

SHE MAY WEAR RED, THE SILK FALLING IN A SOFT CAS-
cade over her shoulder and shimmering with golden embroidery,
her neck adorned with gold and pearls, her arms filigreed with
henna patterns as old as the oldest woman's memory. When
she drapes the garland of roses and jasmine over her beloved's
head, the guests catch it in her eyes—a glimpse of the mystery,
if only for a moment.

Or there may be chairs, hoisted over the shoulders of a raucous crowd and bobbed up and down, two nervous passengers
gripping their seats and laughing over the folksy music of the
horah. When the guests link arms and circle around, they catch
it in the joy of one another's faces—a glimpse of the mystery, if
only for a moment.

Or there may be bagpipes punctuating every step of the recessional with cacophonous formality, as a cavalcade of tartan marches down the grassy aisle. When the couple, decked with thistles and roses, stops midway for another long kiss, the guests whistle and shout and catch it in the sudden fire in her cheeks—a glimpse of the mystery, if only for a moment.

They may wear black-and-white formal attire saved for this day when the champagne cork finally flies and the cameras flash around them. When the signing is finished, the clerk will catch it in the joyous tears that river down their faces—a glimpse of the mystery, if only for a moment.

There may be a crowning, traditional to an Orthodox ceremony, where two gold crowns are placed on their heads, symbols that "here is the beginning of a small kingdom which can be something like the true Kingdom."[85] When the priest declares, "O Lord and God, crown them with glory and honor," the guests in the cathedral catch it in a glint of light against the gold—a glimpse of kingdom come, if only for a moment.

THIRTY-FIVE

Mystery

This is a profound mystery—but I am
talking about Christ and the church.

—Ephesians 5:32

DAN AND I WERE MARRIED IN THE FALL, AT A BAPTIST church called New Union. We chose the church for practical reasons, as the sanctuary was big enough to house all our guests and was close to the reception venue, but I always take pleasure in seeing the church's name embossed in crimson on the framed invitation in our hallway. I wonder how many other couples marked the start of their new unions in that auspicious place.

When I reached the end of the aisle that day, my feet already aching from the ill-advised white and taupe heals that so perfectly matched the dress, Pastor Doug read from Revelation 19 and 21:

Hallelujah!
  For our Lord God Almighty reigns.
Let us rejoice and be glad
  and give him glory!
For the wedding of the Lamb has come,
  and his bride has made herself ready . . .
Blessed are those who are invited to the wedding supper of
  the Lamb!

Then I saw "a new heaven and a new earth . . . I saw the Holy City, the new Jerusalem, coming down out of heaven from God, prepared as a bride beautifully dressed for her husband. And I heard a loud voice from the throne saying, "Look! God's dwelling place is now among the people, and he will dwell with them. They will be his people, and God himself will be with them and be their God. 'He will wipe every tear from their eyes. There will be no more death' or mourning or crying or pain, for the old order of things has passed away." He who was seated on the throne said, "I am making everything new!"

And for a moment, we glimpsed the Great Mystery.

We married before Pinterest, so there were no photo booths or mason jars or mustaches-on-sticks at the reception. Back in those days, the photographer just lined everybody up at the front of the church sanctuary like it was a firing range and took the shot. We didn't even think to pose inside a vintage mirror frame or sit on a rusty pickup truck. But even though we started out young and poor and Republican, our marriage has been a happy one, and has made the meandering journey in and out of church a less lonely one for sure.

Like most Christian couples, our engagement and first year

brought on an avalanche of Christian marriage books, some more helpful than others. Of the unhelpful ones, the worst were those that began with sweeping generalizations about the differences between men and women, then prescribed strict, gender-based roles based on those generalizations. This was usually followed by an appeal to Scripture to support patriarchy, but of the "softer" type, in which the husband does not *own* the wife per se, but does in fact get to choose the restaurants they eat at and the churches they attend. According to these books, if everyone follows the rules and plays their roles—if the right person leads (the man) and the right person follows (the woman), if one person makes the money (the man) and the other person keeps the home (the woman), if there is one protector (the man) and one nurturer (the woman)—then everything will work out.

But what Dan and I found within just a few months of living together is that marriage isn't about sticking to a script; it's about making a life together. It's not a choreographed cha-cha, it's an intimate slow dance. It isn't a formula, it's a mystery. Few of these Christian marriage books prepared us for the actual adventure of marriage, which involves improvisation, compromise, and learning as you go.

Even the apostle Paul, himself single and an enthusiastic proponent of singleness, said as much in his letter to the Ephesians. "Husbands ought to love their wives as their own bodies," he wrote. "He who loves his wife loves himself. After all, no one ever hated their own body, but they feed and care for their body, just as Christ does the church—for we are members of his body . . . This is a profound mystery—but I am talking about Christ and the church" (Ephesians 5:28–30, 32).

Ironically, this very letter is often invoked to support hierarchal gender roles in marriage, because earlier, in urging all members of a household to "submit to one another out of reverence for Christ," Paul describes a typical first-century Greco-Roman household, complete with a male head-of-house who has authority over his wives, slaves, and children. In the past, some Christians referred to this passage to argue that the hierarchy between master and slave is God-ordained, and in the present, some continue to use it to argue that hierarchy between men and women is God-ordained.

But the point of this passage, and of the other New Testament household codes, is not to emphasize the holiness of a single household structure, but rather to admonish Christians to imitate Jesus, no matter where they stand in the sociological pecking order. So men are told to be kind to their slaves, gentle with their children, and loving with their wives (Ephesians 5:25–28; 6:4, 9). Slaves are admonished to work well, with ultimate allegiance to God and with the suffering of Christ as a comfort in their affliction (6:5). Wives and husbands are encouraged to submit to one another in respect, love, and patience with the sacrificial love of Christ as their example (5:21–33).

Paul is not arguing that the first-century Greco-Roman household structure is the best for human flourishing and therefore God's design for all people everywhere. Such a question was not within his purview. Rather, he is explaining that when Christians imitate Jesus in their relationships, when partners in marriage serve one another rather than fight for dominance, we catch a little glimpse of the mystery of Christ's relentless, self-giving love for the church, and the consummation of that love that is to come.

Marriage is not an inherently holy institution. And it cannot magically be made so by the government, by a priest, or even by the church. Rather, marriage is a relationship that is made holy, or sacramental, when it reflects the life-giving, self-sacrificing love of Jesus. All relationships and vocations—marriage, friendship, singleness, parenthood, partnership, ministry, monastic vows, adoption, neighborhoods, families, churches—give Christians the opportunity to reflect the grace and peace of the kingdom of God, however clumsily, however imperfectly. For two people to commit themselves not simply to marriage, but to a lifetime of mutual love and submission in imitation of Christ is so astounding, so mysterious, it comes close to looking like Jesus' stubborn love for the church.

Writes Alexander Schmemann, "We must understand that the real theme, 'content' and object of this sacrament is not 'family,' but love . . . Some of us are married and some are not. Some of us are called to be priests and ministers and some are not. But the sacraments of matrimony and priesthood concern all of us, because they concern our life as vocation. The meaning, the essence and the end of all vocation is the mystery of Christ and the Church."[86]

Marriage, like a meal of bread and wine, is just one more ordinary, everyday circumstance God transforms into an avenue through which to enter our lives. We must be careful, then, of idolizing the *institution* of marriage on the one hand and discounting its kingdom-reflecting potential on the other. What makes a marriage holy isn't the degree to which the two partners reflect gender stereotypes, or stick to a list of rules and roles, or even reflect cultural norms and expectations, but the degree to which the love of Christ is present in one of the most challenging and rewarding commitments two people will ever make to one another.

Just as there is something about bread and wine that reminds us of Jesus' humanity, there is something about the tension and longing of romantic love that reminds us of our desire for God and God's desire for us. Scripture employs this metaphor throughout both the Old and New Testaments, where the relationship between God and God's people is often pictured as a marriage, a covenant of fidelity and love made first with Israel and then with the whole world through the church. The longing of God is captured in a beautiful, oft-repeated refrain woven throughout the pages of Scripture from Exodus to Revelation—"I will give them a heart to know me, that I am the LORD. They will be my people, and I will be their God, for they will return to me with all their heart" (Jeremiah 24:7).

When the people of God abandoned the covenant of love and fidelity, drawn as we are by the appeal of shallow, empty pleasures, God removed every possible obstruction to the covenant by being faithful *for* us, by becoming like us and subjecting himself to the very worst within us, loving us all the way to the cross and all the way out of the grave. In this metaphor, Christ is like a bridegroom who has chosen the church as his bride, and is busy preparing for a great wedding after which their love will be consummated. At the wedding, all the guests will sing, "God's dwelling place is now among the people, and he will dwell with them. They will be his people, and God himself will be with them and be their God."

One can only get so far in thinking all this through before the metaphor breaks down and the meaning becomes obscured. That's okay. It is only a metaphor, and like all metaphors, it isn't the moon, but rather the finger pointing at the moon. We're talking about the Great Mystery here, the ultimate reality that the apostle Paul says we only "see through a mirror dimly" anyway. I may be wrong, but I think the point is this: what each of us longs for the most is to be both fully known and fully loved.[87] Miraculously, God feels the same way about us. God, too, wants to be fully known and fully loved. God wants this so much that he has promised to knock down every obstacle in the way, enduring even his own death, to be with us, to consummate this love. And so, in those relationships and in those moments when we experience the joy, ecstasy, and relief of being both totally vulnerable and absolutely cherished, we get just a taste, a mere glimpse, of what God has always felt for us, and what one day we will feel for God.

The Orthodox Church illustrates all of this quite beautifully in its tradition of crowning the couple in a wedding ceremony.

As Orthodox priest Alexander Schmemann explains, the rite of matrimony consists of two distinct services: the betrothal and the crowning. The betrothal occurs not in the church sanctuary, but in the vestibule, the part of the building that is closest to the outside world as an acknowledgment of the social and legal dimensions of marriage. The couple exchanges rings and their marriage is blessed by the priest. Then, they are invited into the church in a solemn and momentous processional.

"This is the true form of the sacrament," writes Schmemann, "for it does not merely symbolize, but indeed is the entrance of marriage into the Church, which is the entrance of the world into the 'world to come,' the procession of the people of God—in Christ—into the Kingdom."[88]

Once the couple is in the church, they are crowned. Typically, the crowns are identical—(one is not bigger than the other; the "rule" of this new household is to be shared)—and held for a moment over the couple's heads by their attendants while the priest declares, "O Lord and God, crown them with glory and honor!"

The crowns represent the reality that every family is like a little kingdom, and that little kingdom can represent the kingdom of Jesus—where the first is last and the last is first, where the poor and the sick are welcomed in, where the peacemakers and the merciful find a home, where humility and self-sacrifice reign.

"This is what the marriage crowns express," writes Schmemann, "that here is the beginning of a small kingdom which can be something like the true Kingdom. The chance will be lost perhaps even in one night; but at this moment it is still an open possibility. Yet even when it has been lost, and lost again a thousand times, still if two people stay together they are in a real sense king and queen to each other."[89]

Then, after some prayers are prayed and words are spoken, the priest removes the crowns from the heads of the newlyweds and presents them at the altar.

"Receive their crowns in Thy Kingdom," he prays.

Now the crowns invite the couple, their attendants, their families, the priest, the guests, and indeed even God who is present at this wedding, too, to remember "that ultimate Reality of which everything in 'this world'—whose fashion passeth away—everything has now become a sacramental sign and anticipation."[90] Together they catch a glimpse of the Mystery.

Dan and I have been married for eleven years now. Sometimes our marriage looks like the kingdom. Sometimes it does not. Sometimes we wear our crowns with decorum and grace. Sometimes we fight to snatch them off each other's heads. But what makes our marriage holy, what makes it "set apart" and sacramental, isn't the marriage certificate filed away in the basement or the degree to which we follow a list of rules and roles, it's the way God shows up in those everyday moments—loading the dishwasher, sharing a joke, hosting a meal, enduring an illness, working through a disagreement—and gives us the chance to notice, to *pay attention* to the divine. It's the way the God of resurrection makes all things new.

THIRTY-SIX

Body

You are the body of Christ, and each one of you is a part of it.

—1 Corinthians 12:27

"THE CHURCH IS A WHORE, BUT SHE IS MY MOTHER."

The quote is attributed to St. Augustine, but no one's really tracked it down. I'd venture to guess it originated with a man, though, and an unimaginative one at that.

It's not that I don't appreciate the sentiment—that despite her persistent wanderings and betrayals, the church births us and feeds us and names us children of God—it' s just that when we leave men to draw all the theological conclusions about a metaphorically feminine church, we end up with rather predictable categories, don't we?

Virgin. Whore. Mother.

But what might a *woman* say about church as *she*? What might a woman say about the church as body and bride?

Perhaps she would speak of the way a regular body moves through the world—always changing, never perfect—capable of nurturing life, not simply through the womb, but through hands, feet, eyes, voice, and brain. Every part is sacred. Every part has a function.

Perhaps she would speak of impossible expectations and all the time she's wasted trying to contort herself into the shape of those amorphous silhouettes that flit from magazines and billboards into her mind. Or of this screwed-up notion of purity as a status, as something awarded by men with tests and checklists and the power to give it and take it away.

Perhaps she would speak of the surprise of seeing herself—flaws and all—in the mirror on her wedding day. Or of the reality that with new life comes swollen breasts, dry heaves, dirty diapers, snotty noses, late-night arguments, and a whole army of new dangers and fears she never even considered before because life-giving isn't nearly as glamorous as it sounds, but it's a thousand times more beautiful.

Perhaps she would talk about being underestimated, about surprising people and surprising herself. Or about how there are moments when her own strength startles her, and moments when her weakness—her forgetfulness, her fear, her exhaustion—unnerve her.

Maybe she would tell of the time, in the mountains with bare feet on the ground, she stood tall and wise and felt every cell in her body smile in assent as she inhaled and exhaled and in one loud second realized, *I'm alive! I'm enfleshed!* only to forget it the next.

Or maybe she would explain how none of the categories created for her sum her up or capture her essence.

If the church is like a body, like a bride, then perhaps we ought to take her through what Barbara Brown Taylor calls the "spiritual practice of wearing skin":

Whether you are sick or well, lovely or irregular, there comes a time when it is vitally important to your spiritual health to drop your clothes, look in the mirror, and say, "Here I am. This is the body-like-no-other that my life has shaped. I live here. This is my soul's address." After you have taken a good look around, you may decide that there is a lot to be thankful for, all things considered. Bodies take real beatings. That they heal from most things is an underrated miracle. That they give birth is beyond reckoning.[91]

"When I do this," she says, "I generally decide that it is time to do a better job of wearing my skin with gratitude instead of loathing."

So let's turn the mirror:

This is the church. Here she is. Lovely, irregular, sometimes sick and sometimes well. This is the body-like-no-other that God has shaped and placed in the world. Jesus lives here; this is his soul's address. There is a lot to be thankful for, all things considered. She has taken a beating, the church. Every day she meets the gates of hell and she prevails. Every day she serves, stumbles, injures, and repairs. That she has healed is an underrated miracle. That she gives birth is beyond reckoning. Maybe it's time to make peace with her. Maybe it's time to embrace her, flawed as she is.

Maybe it's time to smile back.

Sometimes I think the biggest challenge in talking about the church is telling ourselves the truth about it—acknowledging the scars, staring down the ugly bits, marveling at its resiliency, and believing that this flawed and magnificent body is enough, for now, to carry us through the world and into the arms of Christ.

Perhaps there is more to the church than mother and whore. And perhaps we might learn this from a woman.

THIRTY-SEVEN

Kingdom

Faith comes from listening to the right stories.

—Michael Gungor

JESUS DIDN'T TALK MUCH ABOUT THE CHURCH, BUT HE talked a lot about the kingdom.

The kingdom is like a tiny mustard seed, he said, that grows into an enormous tree with branches wide and strong enough to make a home for all the birds. It is like a buried treasure, a delicious feast, or a net that catches an abundance of fish. The kingdom is right here, Jesus said. It is present and yet hidden, immanent yet transcendent. The kingdom isn't some far-off place you go when you die; the kingdom is at hand—among us and beyond us, now and not-yet. It is the wheat growing in the midst of weeds, the yeast working its magic in the dough, the pearl germinating in a sepulchral shell. It can come and go in the twinkling of an eye, Jesus said. So *pay attention; don't miss it.*

In contrast to every other kingdom that has been and ever will be, this kingdom belongs to the poor, Jesus said, and to the peacemakers, the merciful, and those who hunger and thirst for God. In this kingdom, the people from the margins and the bottom rungs will be lifted up to places of honor, seated at the best spots at the table. This kingdom knows no geographic boundaries, no political parties, no single language or culture. It advances not through power and might, but through acts of love and joy and peace, missions of mercy and kindness and humility. This kingdom has arrived, not with a trumpet's sound but with a baby's cries, not with the vanquishing of enemies but with the forgiving of them, not on the back of a warhorse but on the back of a donkey, not with triumph and a conquest but with a death and a resurrection.

And yet there is more to this kingdom that is still to come, Jesus said, and so we await a day when every tear will be wiped from every eye, when justice will roll down like a river and righteousness like a never-ending stream, when people from every tribe and tongue and nation will live together in peace, when there will be no more death.

There is nothing Jesus talked about more than the good news of this kingdom. He speaks of it more than a hundred times in the Gospels, and only mentions church twice. And yet as nearly every astute reader of Scripture will notice, the opposite is true in the book of Acts and especially the Epistles, where *ekklesia*—the Greek word for *assembly* we translate into *church*—appears hundreds of times with direct references to the kingdom all but absent. Wilhelm Dilthey puts it rather starkly: "Jesus came announcing the Kingdom of God, but what appeared was the church."

There are of course good reasons for the literary discrepancy. The Epistles are, after all, letters, and so they have a pastoral emphasis rather than an evangelistic one. The authors of the epistles are less concerned with announcing the reign of

Jesus to the world and more concerned with working out the details of living together in community with those who have already embraced that reign.[92] The letters of Peter, Paul, James, and John may not speak often of the kingdom, but they speak often of Jesus Christ—the embodiment of that kingdom—and they give us a glimpse into what it was like for the first followers of Jesus to try and apply his teachings to their specific circumstances. (It was, by all accounts, a messy, wild, and beautiful process, riddled with ups and downs and mistakes.)

Still, when we consider all the messes the church has made throughout history, all the havoc she has wreaked and the things she has destroyed, when we face up to just how different the church looks from the kingdom most of the time, it's easy to think maybe Jesus left us with a raw deal. Maybe he pulled a bait and switch, selling us on the kingdom and then slipping us the church.

When I was debating titles for this book, I asked for help on social media, and one reader suggested this: *Jesus Went Back to Heaven and All He Left Me Was This Lousy Church.* That one got a lot of "likes," and I have to admit I can relate.

And yet Jesus made a point of telling Peter—you know, the guy who convinced himself he could walk on water and then sank, who tried to talk Jesus out of his Passion and was rebuked for channeling Satan, who took a sword to the ear of a Roman soldier even after Jesus had been preaching peace for three years, who pretended he didn't even know Jesus when things went south, and who denied Jesus not only once but three times, you know, *that Peter*—he was just the sort of person Jesus wanted use to start his church (Matthew 16:18).

This word for church, *ekklesia*, was used at the time of Jesus to refer to the "calling out" of citizens for a civic meeting or for battle, and is employed in one form or another in both the Old and New Testaments to refer to the people of God, assembled together. So church is, essentially, a gathering of kingdom citizens, called out—from their individuality, from their sins, from their old ways of doing things, from the world's way of doing things—into participation in this new kingdom and community with one another.

I'm not exactly sure how all this works, but I think, ultimately, it means I can't be a Christian on my own. Like it or not, following Jesus is a group activity, something we're supposed to do together. We might not always do it within the walls of church or even in an organized religion, but if we are to go about making disciples, confessing our sins, breaking bread, paying attention, and preaching the Word, we're going to need one another. We're going to need each other's help.

The church is not the same as the kingdom. As George Eldon Ladd explains, "The Kingdom is God's reign and the realm in which the blessings of this reign are experienced; the church is the fellowship of those who have experienced God's reign and entered into the enjoyment of its blessings."[93] The purpose of the church, and of the sacraments, is to give the world a glimpse of the kingdom, to point in its direction. When we put a kingdom-spin on ordinary things—water, wine, leadership, marriage, friendship, feasting, sickness, forgiveness—we see that they can be holy, they can point us to something greater than ourselves, a fantastic mystery that brings meaning to everything. We make something sacramental when we make it like the kingdom. Marriage is sacramental when it is characterized by mutual love and submission. A meal is sacramental when the rich and poor, powerful and marginalized, sinners and saints share equal status around the table. A local church is sacramental when it is a place where the last are first and the first are last and where those who hunger and thirst are fed. And the church universal is sacramental when it knows no geographic boundaries, no political parties, no single language or culture, and when it advances not through power and might, but through acts of love, joy, and peace and missions of mercy, kindness, humility.

In this sense, church gives us the chance to riff on Jesus' description of the kingdom, to add a few new metaphors of our own. We might say the kingdom is like St. Lydia's in Brooklyn where strangers come together and remember Jesus when they eat. The kingdom is like the Refuge in Denver, where addicts and academics, single moms and suburban housewives come together to tell each other the truth. The kingdom is like Thistle Farms where women heal from abuse by helping to heal others. The kingdom is like the church that would rather die than cast two of its own out the doors because they are gay. The kingdom is like St. Luke's Episcopal Church in Cleveland, Tennessee, where you are loved just for showing up.

And even still, the kingdom remains a mystery just beyond our grasp. It is here, and not yet, present and still to come. Consummation, whatever that means, awaits us. Until then, all we have are metaphors. All we have are *almosts* and *not quites* and wayside shrines. All we have are imperfect people in an imperfect world doing their best to produce outward signs of inward grace and stumbling all along the way.

All we have is this church—this lousy, screwed-up, glorious church—which, by God's grace, is enough.

Dark

Not knowing when the dawn will come I open every door.

—Emily Dickinson

WE HAVE COME TO THE FINAL CHAPTER, AND I WRITE IT, appropriately enough, just before dawn on a Sunday morning. The house is quiet and the windows are dark. Dan snores in the room across the hall while I patter away at the keyboard, one last all-nighter before I finally send this book to the publisher. There's this mockingbird that's been singing from about midnight to three in the morning like she's got the New York Philharmonic behind her, and I can't for the life of me figure out what's up with her, if singing loud into the night while the rest of the world roosts means she's got some sort of malfunction of the brain or if it means she knows something important about the darkness that the rest of don't. *I wonder what she sees.*

But even the mockingbird has grown silent at this dark, heavy hour when the night stretches out like an inky ocean and it's hard to remember the colors of day. I find myself wondering if perhaps every generation of Christians has felt itself at the

257

edge of this precipice, waiting for resurrection and worrying it might not come. Perhaps every pilgrim in search of church has wondered if it's a lifetime of feeling his way through the dark, longing for light.

But if I've learned anything in this journey, both in writing this book and clumsily living its content, it's that Sunday morning sneaks up on us—like dawn, like resurrection, like the sun that rises a ribbon at a time. We expect a trumpet and a triumphant entry, but as always, God surprises us by showing up in ordinary things: in bread, in wine, in water, in words, in sickness, in healing, in death, in a manger of hay, in a mother's womb, in an empty tomb. Church isn't some community you join or some place you arrive. Church is what happens when someone taps you on the shoulder and whispers in your ear, *Pay attention, this is holy ground; God is here.*

Even here, in the dark, God is busy making all things new.

So show up. Open every door. At the risk of looking like a fool buried with his feet facing the East or like a mockingbird singing stubbornly at the night, anticipate resurrection. It's either just around the bend or a million miles away. Or perhaps it's somewhere in between.

Let's find out together.

Acknowledgments

My research for this book, more than any other, revealed the degree to which I am indebted to wise and faithful women whose insights into the meaning of baptism, communion, confession, and healing shaped so much of the content of this book. I turned to Nora Gallagher, Sara Miles, Barbara Brown Taylor, and Nadia Bolz-Weber again and again and was always freshly surprised by their profound grasp of grace.

Thanks also to my friends Shauna Niequist and Rachel Marie Stone, whose insights into food and table shaped much of the content of the Communion section, and to Heather Kopp, Kathy Escobar, Becca Stevens, Christena Cleveland, and Glennon Melton, who are teaching so many of us to tell the truth.

I devoured every word of Alexander Schmemann's *For the Life of the World* and Justo Gonzalez's *The Story of Christianity*, both of which provided direction and ideas for this project. And I am as indebted as ever to Brian McLaren, who inspires both with his words and his life.

Thanks to Ann Voskamp for the orchids, and Glennon Melton, Sarah Bessey, Kristen Howerton, Jen Hatmaker, Jamie Wright, and Tara Livesay for the dinner and wine. Thanks to the brilliant Preston Yancey who read an early version of this book and assured me I wasn't crazy.

I am more grateful than ever for Chris and Tiffany Hoose, who have stuck with our friendship through such a busy season, and for Mom, Dad, Amanda, and Tim for loving me so well through yet another creative project. There are not enough thank-yous in the world for Dan, whose tireless support, compassion, and good humor I too often take for granted.

Writing this book forever changed how I look at my own church story and the people who influenced it. I hope I managed to capture my abiding love and appreciation for Brian and Carrie Ward, who have perhaps shaped my faith more than any other couple besides my parents and whose friendship and example has change my life. I am grateful, too, for the communities of Faith Chapel, Grace Bible Church, and St. Luke's Episcopal Church and for all they have taught me about Jesus.

Thanks, of course, to my brilliant literary agent Rachelle Gardner—the perfect teammate and a good friend. And thanks to my booking agent, Jim Chaffee, for supporting me, challenging me, and, most importantly, cooking for me.

There is no better publishing team than my team at Thomas Nelson—Brian Hampton, Kristen Parrish, Chad Cannon, Stephanie Tresner, Belinda Bass, Emily Lineberger, Heather Skelton, and my copyeditor, Jamie Chavez. Your work on both this project and the last one has made collaboration a complete joy. Thanks especially for your patience.

Thanks to all the people who responded to my random Facebook questions about theology and church, especially Stephen Mckinney-Whitaker, who came up with the title for this book, and Stanley Helton, Steve Schaefer, Jen Rogers, and Ray Hollenbach, who helped me figure out the kingdom of God at the eleventh hour.

Finally, I owe so much of the opportunity to write and publish to my faithful readers at rachelheldevans.com. Your stories, insights, questions, and pushback shaped the content of this book more than any other. In a way, it feels like we wrote it together. I can't wait to see what we do together next.

Notes

1. Francis, *The Joy of the Gospel: Evangelii Gaudium* (Usccb, 2013), 28.
2. Dietrich Bonhoeffer, *Life Together: The Classic Exploration of Christian Community,* trans. John W. Doberstein (New York: Harper & Row Publishers, 1954), 42.
3. These numbers come from David Kinnaman's excellent book, *You Lost Me: Why Young Christians Are Leaving the Church . . . And Rethinking Faith* (Grand Rapids, MI: Baker Books, 2011) and from "Religion Among the Millennials," the Pew Research Center's Religion and Public Life Project, www.pewforum.org/2010/02/17/religion-among-the-millennials/ (accessed 13 October 2014).
4. See especially Kinnaman, *You Lost Me.*
5. Barbara Brown Taylor, *An Altar in the World* (New York: HarperOne, 2009), 45.
6. Justo Gonzalez, *The Story of Christianity, Volume II: The Reformation to the Present Day* (New York: HarperOne, 2010), 71.
7. William Willimon, *Remember Who You Are: Baptism, A Model for Christian Life* (Nashville, TN: Upper Room Books, 1980), 37.
8. The name of the church was actually Faith Chapel of Huffman, a nondenominational Bible church. However, years after we moved from Birmingham, the congregation changed locations to become Deerfoot Community Bible Church. I changed the name of the church in this book so it would not be confused with Faith Chapel Christian Center, another church in present-day Birmingham.

9. Nadia Bolz-Weber, *Pastrix: The Cranky, Beautiful Faith of a Sinner & Saint* (New York: Jericho, 2013), 138.

10. Sources for the reconstruction of these ancient baptismal practices include: Justo L. Gonzalez, *The Story of Christianity, Volume I: The Early Church to the Dawn of the Reformation* (New York: HarperOne, 2010); Alexander Schmemann, *For the Life of the World* (New York: St. Vladimir's Seminary Press, 1973); and Willimon, *Remember Who You Are.*

11. Schmemann, *For the Life of the World*, 69.

12. Ibid., 71.

13. Willimon, *Remember Who You Are*, 100–101, 103.

14. For these and other stories, see Rachel Held Evans, "It's a wonder any of us survived youth group," December 3, 2013, rachelheldevans. com/blog/youth-group-games (accessed 13 October 2014).

15. Thanks to Brian McLaren for calling this aspect of John's life to my attention in *We Make the Road by Walking: A Year-Long Quest for Spiritual Formation, Reorientation, and Activation* (New York: Jericho, 2014).

16. Associated Press, "Tennessee lawmakers confuse mop sink in State Capitol for Muslim foot-washing sink," *Chattanooga Times Free Press*, March 26, 2013, www.timesfreepress.com/news/2013/mar/26/ tennessee-lawmakers-confuse-mop-sink-state-capitol/ (accessed 13 October 2014).

17. Anne Sexton, *Selected Poems of Anne Sexton*, edited by Diane Wood Middlebrook and Dianna Hume George (Boston: First Mariner Books, 2000).

18. Heather Kopp, *Sober Mercies: How Love CaughtUp With a Christian Drunk* (New York: Jericho, 2013).

19. *The Book of Common Prayer* (New York: Seabury Press, 1979), 82.

20. *Lutheran Book of Worship: Pew Edition* (Minneapolis: Augsburg Fortress, 1978).

21. Nadia Bolz-Weber, "Being Good Doesn't Make You Free. The Truth Makes You Free," *Sojourners*, March 28, 2012, sojo.net/ blogs/2012/03/28/being-good-doesn%E2%80%99t-make-you-free-truth-makes-you-free (accessed 13 October 2014).

22. Bonhoeffer, *Life Together*, 110.

23. Kathy Escobar, *Down We Go: Living Into the Wild Ways of Jesus* (Folson, CA: Civitas Press, 2011), 35.

24. Used with permission from Kathy Escobar and the Refuge community: www.therefugeonline.org/ (accessed 13 October 2014).

25. John Mason, *A Brief History of the Pequot War* (Bedford, MA: Applewood Books, 2009), 81.

26. Mark Noll, *The Civil War as a Theological Crisis* (Chapel Hill: The University of North Carolina Press, 2006), 39.

27. Christopher Connell, "Bob Jones University: Doing Battle in the Name of Religion and Freedom," *Change* 15, no.4 (1983): 41.

28. Erin Conway Smith, "Uganda passes anti-gay bill." *Telegraph*, December 20, 2013, http://www.telegraph.co.uk/news/worldnews/africaandindianocean/uganda/10531563/Uganda-passes-anti-gay-bill.html (accessed 1 November 2014).

29. Thomas Clarkson, *The History of the Rise, Progress, and Accomplishment of the Abolition of the African Slave Trade by the British Parliament* (London: John W. Parker, 1808), 448.

30. *The Book of Common Prayer.*

31. Brennan Manning, *The Ragamuffin Gospel: Good News for the Bedraggled, Beat-Up, and Burnt Out* (Sisters, OR: Multnomah Publishers, 2005), 23.

32. In the interest of full disclosure, this paragraph creatively combines our experiences church hunting both before and after our experience with the Mission, which is described in the Holy Orders section of the book.

33. John 8:1–11.

34. *The Book of Common Prayer.*

35. J. R. Briggs, *Fail: Finding Hope and Grace in the Midst of Ministry Failure* (Downers Grove, IL: Intervarsity Press, 2014), 46.

36. Ibid., 21–22.

37. Schmemann, *For the Life of the World*, 93.

38. Barbara Brown Taylor, *Leaving Church: A Memoir of Faith* (New York: Harper One, 2007), 44.

39. Gonzalez, *The Story of Christianity, Volume II*, 107–108.

40. Taylor, *An Altar in the World*, 45.

41. Gonzalez, *The Story of Christianity, Volume II*, 60, 105.

42. Paul Bradshaw, ed., *The New Westminster Dictionary of Liturgy and Worship* (Louisville: John Knox Press, 2003), 136.

43. Nora Gallagher, *The Sacred Meal* (Nashville: Thomas Nelson, 2009), 11.

44. Emily Scott, "Dinner church: sit down at the table," *Episcopal Café*, February 3, 2010, www.episcopalcafe.com/daily/evangelism/dinner_church.php (accessed 13 October 2014).

45. Shauna Niequist, *Bread & Wine: A Love Letter to Life Around the Table* (Grand Rapids: Zondervan, 2013), 14.

46. N. T. Wright, *Simply Jesus: A New Vision of Who He Was, What He Did, and Why He Matters* (New York: HarperOne, 2011), 180.

47. Gallagher, *The Sacred Meal*, 45, 46.

48. Robert Farrar Capon, *Between Noon and Three: Romance, Law, and the Outrage of Grace* (Grand Rapids: Eerdmans, 1997), 7.

49. Schmemann, *For the Life of the World*, 45.

50. Sara Miles, *Take This Bread* (New York: Ballantine Books, 2008), 58.

51. Ibid, 60.
52. Ibid.
53. My thanks to Rachel Marie Stone for drawing this to my attention in her excellent book, *Eat With Joy: Redeeming God's Gift of Food* (Downers Grove, IL: Intervarsity Press, 2013), from which I drew much inspiration for this chapter.
54. "Eucharist: The Rt. Rev. Michael Curry," video, 7:50, posted by New Tracts for Our Times, June 6, 2014, https://www.youtube.com/watch?v=USOMZpGheBc (accessed 2 November 2014).
55. Richard Beck, *Unclean: Meditations on Purity, Hospitality, and Mortality* (Eugene, OR: Cascade Books, 2011), 114.
56. Robert E. Webber, *Evangelicals on the Canterbury Trail: Why Evangelicals Are Attracted to the Liturgical Church* (Harrisburg, PA: Morehouse Publishing, 1985), 45.
57. Milton Brasher-Cunningham, *Keeping the Feast: Metaphors for the Meal* (Harrisburg: Morehouse Publishing, 2012), 38.
58. Susan Heller Anderson and David W. Dunlap, "New York Day by Day; Author to Readers," *The New York Times*, April 25, 1985, http://www.nytimes.com/1985/04/25/nyregion/new-york-day-by-day-author-to-readers.html (accessed 3 November 2014).
59. If you were paying attention, you spotted images related to the six Holy Spirit similes found in the previous chapter—breath, fire, seal, bird, wind, and womb—in this chapter.
60. Walker Percy, *The Moviegoer* (New York: Vintage, 1998), 13.
61. Rachel Sussman, *The Oldest Living Things in the World* (Chicago: The University of Chicago Press, 2014), 55.
62. John R. Franke, *Manifold Witness: The Plurality of Truth* (Nashville: Abington Press, 2009), 136.
63. William James, "The Confidences of a Psychial Researcher," *The American Magazine* (Volume 68: May–October, 1909), 589.
64. *Catechism of the Catholic Church*, (Vatican: Liberia Editrice Vaticana, 2000), 1302–1303.
65. Lauren Winner, *Still: Notes on a Mid-Faith Crisis* (New York: Harper One, 2013).
66. Sara Miles, *Jesus Freak: Feeding, Healing, Raising the Dead* (San Francisco, CA: Jossey Bass, 2010), 11.
67. Check out the Momastery community's amazing Love Flash Mobs here: momastery.com/blog/category/love-flash-mobs/ (accessed 13 October 2014).
68. Exodus 30:34–38, Leviticus 6:15, Psalm 45:8, Psalm 51:7, Song of Solomon 4:13–14, John 12:3–5, John 19:39–42, Revelation 5:8.
69. 1 John 2:20, 2 Corinthians 2:15.

70. Catholic Church, *Catechism of the Catholic Church. 2nd ed.* (Vatican: Libreria Editrice Vaticana, 2000), 1527.
71. Names and some identifying details changed to protect privacy.
72. Miles, *Jesus Freak*, 105.
73. "Brene Brown: Jesus Wept," video, 6:00, *The Work of the People*, www.theworkofthepeople.com/jesus-wept (accessed 13 October 2014).
74. Be sure to check out the amazing products from Thistle Farms—a great way to support an organization changing lives through education, entrepreneurship, and love: www.thistlefarms.org/ (accessed 13 October 2014).
75. Becca Stevens, *Snake Oil: The Art of Healing and Truth-Telling* (Nashville: Jericho Books, 2013), 49.
76. Ibid.,140.
77. Names and some details have been changed in this account, for privacy purposes.
78. Laurie Goodstein, "Christian Charity Backtracks on Gays," *New York Times*, March 27, 2014, www.nytimes.com/2014/03/28/us/christian-charity-backtracks-on-gays.html?_r=0 (accessed 13 October 2014).
79. Diana Butler Bass, *Christianity After Religion: The End of Church and the Birth of a New Spiritual Awakening* (New York: HarperOne, 2012), 13.
80. "Six Reasons Young Christians Leave Church," The Barna Group, September 28, 2011, www.barna.org/teens-next-gen-articles/528-six-reasons-young-christians-leave-church (accessed 13 October 2014).
81. G. K. Chesterton, *The Everlasting Man* (New York: EMP Books, 2012), 213.
82. Cheryl M. Lawrence, "A good death," *Faith & Leadership*, April 22, 2014, www.faithandleadership.com/content/cheryl-m-lawrence-good-death (accessed 13 October 2014).
83. Stacey Chomiak, "The Church That Loved," February 4, 2014, rachelheldevans.com/blog/church-loved (accessed 13 Octobr 2014).
84. Barbara Brown Taylor, *Learning to Walk in the Dark* (New York: HarperOne, 2014), 129.
85. From the account of a traditional Orthodox crowing in Schmemann, *For the Life of the World*, 89.
86. Ibid., 82.
87. Tim Keller uses similar language in his book, *The Meaning of Marriage* (New York: Riverhead, 2011).
88. Schmemann, *For the Life of the World*, 89.
89. Ibid.
90. Ibid., 91.

91. Taylor, *An Altar in the World*, 38.
92. Thanks to the wonderful Diana Butler Bass, who explained this to me via a Facebook conversation because she is awesome.
93. George Eldon Ladd, *The Presence of the Future* (Grand Rapids: Wm. B. Eerdmans, 1974), 262.

About the Author

Rachel Held Evans, an award-winning writer, is a popular blogger and the author of *Faith Unraveled* and the *New York Times* best-selling *A Year of Biblical Womanhood*. She lives in Dayton, TN.